"Take, Read"

ALSO BY WESLEY A. KORT

Shriven Selves: Religious Problems in Recent American Fiction (1972)

Narrative Elements and Religious Meaning (1975)

Moral Fiber: Character and Belief in Recent American Fiction (1982)

Modern Fiction and Human Time: A Study of Narrative and Belief (1985)

Story, Text, and Scripture: Literary Interests in Biblical Narrative (1988)

Bound to Differ: The Dynamics of Theological Discourses (1992)

WESLEY A. KORT

"TAKE, READ"

Scripture, Textuality,
and Cultural Practice

The Pennsylvania State University Press
University Park, Pennsylvania

Library of Congress Cataloging-in-Publication Data

Kort, Wesley A.
    Take, Read : Scripture, textuality, and cultural practice / Wesley A. Kort.
        p.   cm.
    Includes bibliographical references and index.
    ISBN 0-271-01591-8 (alk. paper)
    ISBN 0-271-01592-6 (pbk. : alk. paper)
    1. Bible—Evidences, authority, etc.   2. Bible—Reading.
    3. Bible—Hermeneutics.   4. Criticism.   I. Title.
    BS480.K64   1996
    220.1—dc20
                                                                            95-48947
                                                                            CIP

It is the policy of The Pennsylvania State University Press to use acid-free paper for
the first printing of all clothbound books. Publications on uncoated stock satisfy the
minimum requirements of American National Standard for Information Sciences–
Permanence of Paper for Printed Library Materials, ANSI Z39.48-1992.

For Patrick and Dennis Rankowitz

And suddenly I heard a voice from a nearby house chanting and repeating over and over—whether a boy's or girl's voice, I do not know: "Take, read; take, read."

—Saint Augustine's *Confessions*, bk. 8, chap. 12

CONTENTS

ACKNOWLEDGMENTS

I did most of the preparatory work for this book and got a good start on writing it during two stays at the Center of Theological Inquiry in Princeton, N.J., the fall semester of 1992 and the winter of 1994. I am grateful to the Center for its support, to the director, Dan Hardy, for his intelligent encouragement of the project, and to other scholars in residence during those two periods, especially Peter Ochs, for their responses to presentations of work in progress. I am also grateful to friends at other institutions who read earlier versions of the book and gave helpful suggestions, especially Philip Rolnick at Greensboro College and Terrence Tilley at the University of Dayton. I am grateful also for the interest a few of my colleagues here at Duke have shown in my work, two of whom read parts of the manuscript, Willie Jennings and Mary McClintock Fulkerson. And I am thankful for good listeners and interlocutors at home, my wife Phyllis and our daughter, Eva Deane.

INTRODUCTION
"Scripture" as a Category in Textual Theory

At one time people knew what it meant to read a text as scripture, but we no longer do, because this way of reading has, since the late medieval and reformation periods, been dislocated and obscured. This dislocation has been so thorough that it is difficult today to know how to raise the prospect of reading a text as scripture, to regain a sense of what such a practice would be like, why it should be engaged, and what difference it would make. It is not as though the once wide cultural recognition of this practice has slowly, over the centuries, been confined to particular religious communities; the context and occasion of reading do not guarantee that a text will be read as scripture, and religious communities, if they are different from the general culture, have not established that difference on a certain reading practice. Theological treatments of biblical texts or doctrines of Scripture will provide no resource for this project either, because theologies and doctrines determine reading more than they are determined by it. Finally, little help is likely to come from the theories of textuality and of reading that form a conspicuous part of literary studies these days, since these theories generally are extensions of the cultural move away from reading a text as scripture. No, an understanding of what it would be like to read a text as scripture must be recovered and reconstructed, and an effort toward recovering and reconstructing this particular way of reading will be attempted in this study.

I begin by describing what it meant to read a text as scripture in the period immediately preceding modernity. I then try to trace what happened to that practice of reading in the modern period; in a word, I believe that it was transferred from the reading of biblical texts to the reading of nature, then to reading history, and finally to reading literature. I then point out why reading a text as scripture is a practice contrary to the flow of interests that mark our own, postmodernist situation and why reading scripture could address some of the lacks in this cultural context. Then I look at the work of two theorists, Maurice Blanchot and Julia Kristeva, as sites where the faint, unrecognized reappearance of reading texts as scripture occurs. At the end, I address the possibility, following the directions implicit in Blanchot and Kristeva, of reading the Bible as though it were scripture.

The topic of this study is not a matter only of historical interest or of relevance only to some individuals or communities in our culture. Rather, it is a matter of general importance because reading a text as scripture is crucial to an adequate textual or cultural theory. In other words, the question what it would be like to read a text as scripture is relevant to the topics of individual and group identity and the sense that people have of living in a significant world and acting meaningfully within it. The category of scripture and what it is like to read a text as scripture are, I argue, indispensable to cultural studies. Before turning to the question of reading a text as scripture, therefore, I shall point out two reasons why the category of scripture, rather than a topic of occasional or optional interest, is requisite to an adequate textual theory. After placing the category of scripture in textual and cultural studies, I turn, in the body of this project, toward the question of reading scripture as a cultural practice.

I

The first contribution that a category of "scripture" makes to textual theory is to provide and indicate location on the textual field. While every participant of a culture—persons, groups, and institutions—has its identity in relation to the textual field of which that culture is constituted, no participant can include that entire field or be everywhere or simply anywhere on it. Each participant at any time has a particular textual location and relations of similarity and difference to the locations of other participants in the culture. This does not mean that participants have only one location, although it can be said that as the category of scripture is applied to cultural participants, it will designate less variety of texts as one moves from individuals to groups and finally to institutions.

The relations of people to their textual locations are complicated by many factors. For example, locations are both chosen and imposed, are both actively and passively possessed, and are both consciously and unconsciously held. The many contributing factors in the formation of location lie beyond the scope of this study. The principal point to be made here is simply that individuals, groups, and institutions have rather specific and recognizable locations on the textual field, and the category of scripture serves a textual theory by taking that fact into account.

People have locations on the textual field because assumptions, norms, and values give their worlds certain shapes, limits, and coloration and warrant, direct, and correct how they deport themselves in those worlds. These constituting and enabling beliefs are actually or potentially inscribed, and the implicit or explicit texts of these beliefs are the scriptures of individuals, groups, and institutions. Because the texts that constitute a person's scriptures are primary for the world they support, those texts hold the potential to sustain or reconfigure that world when it has in part been disconfirmed or at points found to be unsatisfying or unworkable. Beliefs are inscribed and derived from texts in order to construct or project worlds and to correct or reconfirm them. "Scripture," then, functions as a category in textual and cultural theory to designate the locations of persons, groups, and institutions on the textual field.

Having made this point, I want to anticipate two rejoinders. The first is that the category of scripture invalidates the important cultural distinction between norms and judgments that are based on personal, group, or institutional interests and those that are impartial and generally applicable. Rather than invalidate this distinction, I would point out that the category of impartial judgments is not separate from but is itself related to the scriptures of persons, groups, or institutions. The belief that some norms and judgments—scholarly or legal, for example—are constant and without regard to particular values and interests is a location-granting belief inscribed in the texts of some institutions that makes certain kinds of occasions and actions possible. The value imputed to impartial norms and judgments is textually stabilized and culturally specific.

The second rejoinder, once made to me by a colleague, is that a cultural theory that makes textuality so basic and determining is a theory that drains reality from culture, that grants existence to texts alone. My reply is that while we cannot be free from the texts that constitute our culture, this does not mean that the texts of belief cut us off from actuality. The category of scripture need not put us wholly out of touch with the non- or not-yet-textual. We do not, to change the language, live only in the texts of memory and anticipation, only in the past and the future. We also live in the present, but we do not live in a present unaffected by the texts of anticipation and memory. The value and force of present time or of actuality will be variously posited by differing scriptures, however; for many people in our culture, including my colleague, present time has an extremely high value. Other cultures or other people in our culture may discount the importance of the present by stressing the texts of the future or of the past. In the face of this range of belief about the present, it can be said, however loosely, that we neither live in present time cut off from the texts of future and past nor live wholly and necessarily cut off from the present. Present time, as Saint Augustine pointed out, is both the only real time and a time to which we cannot refer. In other words, textual theory need not challenge the crucial assumptions of ordinary language, namely, that when we speak about the world, hearers can assume that we take the world actually to be as we describe or refer to it, and that when we speak about the world, we believe that what we are saying is relevant to it or is true or is both.

However, to make the claim that every person, group, and institution has scriptures also is to invite objections from those who have taken the linguistic and textual turns in cultural studies. They will reject the category of scripture as depending on now discredited theories of textual coherence. Theorists influenced by Jacques Derrida particularly and by deconstruction generally will argue that the category of textual location can only be deployed by someone who still operates with notions of textual particularity and autonomy that recent theory and practice have dismissed. They will argue that the cultural situation is constituted by signifiers that, by their dependence on one another, subvert the separability of specific textual locations. If the textual field militates against the possibility of particularity, of texts standing out as identifiable, the category of scripture evaporates or is dissolved in and by the textual field. Locations, for those voicing this objection, are determined not by texts that grant significance and even coherence to the worlds of people but by the exercise of power that allows people to seize some locations and to impose locations on other people. The category of scripture, the objection continues, conceals the dynamics and consequences of such power plays under the cover of significance. It is, in other words, ideology.

By proposing that every person or group has a scripture, I do not imply a theory of the autonomy and transcendence of particular texts that distinguishes them from or elevates them above the textual field. I agree that texts interpenetrate, derive their significance by dynamics of similarity and difference, and are mutually subversive. This means that all scriptures and the worlds drawn from and sustained by them are partial. They are partial in the sense of not being all-inclusive, and they are partial in the sense of being invested with interests. The scriptures of a person, group, or institution are part of the textual field and are invested with interest and with the force that interests imply and generate. But this force is not something naked that is cloaked in or concealed by language. It is as mistaken to think that force is separable from significance in human affairs as to think that significance, even if in only some of its forms, stands above or apart from the dynamics of power.

To propose a category of scripture for textual theory, finally, is not to stand with people who exempt their own scripture from the dynamics of the textual field, believing that their texts have unique and therefore transcendent properties. True, many for whom the Bible is scripture contend that it is uniquely free from the characteristics of other texts, but it is not. A biblical text has its identity and significance because of dynamics of similarity and difference involving other texts both biblical and nonbiblical. However, this in no way discredits either the force and significance that biblical texts can and do have in the lives of people or the claim of such people that this force and significance in their lives are unique.

What I intend by the category of scripture is a textual designation that stands somewhere between "writing," with its suggestion of nonspecificity and dislocation, and "canon," with its suggestion of autonomy and transcendence. "Scripture" is a category divorced neither from the characteristics of writing nor from the particularizing effects of people's beliefs and identities. The category of scripture avoids both the assumed autonomy, coherence, and permanence of the textual category of canon and the "writing" category's presumption that a person or group can be anywhere or nowhere in particular on the textual field. Indeed, transcendence is assumed by both the advocates of canon and by their deconstructionist counterparts. The former abstract particular texts from their interactive, mutual relations with other texts and impute an unwarranted autonomy to them. The latter, advocates of writing, assume a transcendence to themselves above the limitations and determinations of specific textual locations.

By emphasizing that scripture enables people to have worlds and to act meaningfully within them, I do not mean that scripture has only supportive functions. Scripture also constrains, inhibits, creates fears, and sets limits.

The texts of both the past and of the future, of memory and of expectation, do all of these, although it can generally be said that the texts of memory tend to be more constraining and the texts of the future more evocative of possibility and potential.

Furthermore, by relating scripture to the constitution and maintenance of the worlds people inhabit I do not mean that scripture only constructs and confirms those worlds and the behavior of the people sustained by them. Scriptures also interrogate those worlds and their behavior. True, some scriptures can be seen as doing far more of one than of the other, but in the scriptures of any person, group, or institution there seem to be resources for self-critique as well as for location and confirmation. So, for example, an institution that has grown quite content with its position and activities can be called to task by some neglected parts of its actual or implied scriptures and can be urged to change or improve itself. Conversely, in a therapeutic situation an analysand who has been so disconfirmed by the texts of his or her assumptions and beliefs as to be almost paralyzed can be relocated and reconfirmed by neglected aspects of his or her scriptures that, under the therapist's guidance, can be brought to light.

However, when the category of scripture is used in a textual theory to designate location, emphasis falls more on the construction and confirmation of people's worlds than on their interrogation and disconfirmation. The emphasis shifts in the chapters ahead because the topic of reading a text as scripture more fully engages the process of disconfirming and even dissolving a person's world, position in it, and mode of behavior by means of reading.

While it is my intention, with these remarks, to free the category of scripture from its confinement to specifically religious contexts in order to identify it first of all as part of a general textual or cultural theory, I do not want to minimize the importance of those contexts and of the role of the Bible in providing the scriptures of Western culture generally and of many people specifically today. However, no understanding of scripture in religious contexts is possible without knowing why people have scriptures to begin with, and no doctrine of scripture mounted by a religious group can be adequate unless it takes into account the role of scripture in the culture more broadly. This does not mean that it is necessary or even desirable to force the questions of scripture in religious and nonreligious contexts into the same discourse. While everyone has beliefs and scriptures, not all beliefs and scriptures need be called religious and not all religious beliefs and scriptures need be explained as simply cultural locations. As nonreligious people should recognize that they live with beliefs and scriptures, religious people should recognize that their scriptures are not independent of the broader cultural need to have a scripture and of the dynamics of difference and similarity that grant identity on the textual field. My point about scripture as textual location can be placed between two sets of powerful alternatives: on the one side stands the denial that there can or should be a category of scripture in textual and cultural theory, and on the other stands the claim that the Bible as scripture has nothing to do with the general topic of scripture in textual theory and cultural studies.

It should also be said that the standing of biblical texts as scripture in Western culture generally—and still for many people today—is itself no small ingredient in the formation of the category of scripture for textural theory. The role or standing of a theory of textuality in our culture cannot be dissociated from the prominent and prestigious position of the Bible, however attacked, ignored, or attenuated its influence in modern and postmodern cultures has been.

I would also contend that the Bible continues to serve so well as scripture for some people and has for them survived attack and neglect not only because they have not found suitable alternative scriptures but also because the Bible, even though many of its defenders might fail to realize it, has so many textual characteristics suited to scripture. For example, the Bible, as a collection of many, diverse, and often conflicting texts, has rich variety as well as significant continuities. Its texts represent cultural/historical diversity and arise from a wide range of situations and times. In addition, the Bible contains generic diversity, including narratives, poetry, riddles, letters, proverbs, speeches, and other discursive forms. And it is religiously and theologically diverse (of which more is said below). This great diversity within the limits of a relatively small assemblage of texts, texts that also sustain significant continuities, illustrates the role scripture plays—the beliefs and assumptions it potentially or actually articulates and the identities it grants and questions—in an adequate textual or cultural theory.

In addition, biblical texts are highly intertextual. Biblical texts duplicate or reinforce as well as differ from and even counter one another. Texts from other cultures have been absorbed or rejected, and the histories of specific texts are often complex and layered. Indeed, there seem in the texts themselves fewer attempts to conceal the signs of dependence, combination, and conflict than to let them stand out. All of this gives to the texts a polyphonic quality that institutions dependent on the texts have, because of the value placed by the culture on coherence, treated as a problem or an embarrassment needing to be concealed or transcended. Indeed, biblical diversity is so strong that it has given rise to many differing groups and institutions within both Judaism and Christianity that, often for the sake of coherence, are strongly opposed to one another. So characteristic is this situation that using "Judaism" or "Christianity" in the singular seems hardly defensible.

Finally, biblical texts have served effectively as scriptures because they are so highly transportable. This is because they combine very particular figures, events, and situations with a language of general application. The psalms, for example, although often personal and specific in origin and location, have been used as liturgical and devotional material for believers in almost every imaginable condition. Biblical narratives, while presenting specifically drawn characters, places, and events, have served as metanarratives by which diverse people have allowed their own stories to be shaped. Biblical proverbs, although specific and sharply focused, seem designed to have wide and various applications. Indeed, it seems impossible to encircle the effects of this transportability or to mark out where it ends, and one cannot think of Western culture apart from the storehouse of tropes, plots, and paradigms drawn from biblical texts. To a large extent, either by acts of dependence or by acts of rejection, Western culture can be understood as a long and complex commentary on and reapplication of biblical texts.

I make these comments not so much to advocate the Bible as scripture as to indicate some reasons why the Bible maintains its standing as scripture for many people yet today, to account in part for its continuing tenure and tenacity. Indeed, one could contend that the standing or role of biblical texts in relation to the culture is of more actual and potential consequence for it than is the standing or role of religious institutions or communities, noteworthy as these in many ways are. It is not so much that the texts are important because of institutions or communities as that institutions or communities derive their importance from these texts.

I contend, then, that cultural studies should take into account that persons, groups, and institutions are and can be located on the textual field because they are identified by worlds constituted and sustained by beliefs that have been or could be inscribed. The category of scripture used in that account is deployed between the contraries of writing and canon, and it opposes the transcendence implied or claimed by both sides. I contend both that the denizens of modern and postmodern cultures, whether they like it or not, have scriptures and that the continuing role of the Bible as scripture is to be accounted for at least in part by its textual properties.

II

The first point concerning the category of scripture in textual theory emphasized the matter of location on the textual field; the second turns attention more to the beliefs that grant a person, group, or institution a world and a mode of operating within it. The second point affords a less external and more internal account of the consequences of scripture for constituting and sustaining a world.

A world provides those who inhabit it a set of unmediated relations between events and entities and their significance and value. A person has a world and can carry on in it because there is no need to question, construct, or defend a relation between at least some things or events and their value and meaning. A person has a world because there is no gap between at least some actions, events, or entities and the force and significance they are taken to have or to lack. These relations need not be complete and unchangeable, although what can be left incomplete and what can be taken as changeable are matters also derived from the scriptures that sustain that world.

The scriptures that provide a world and how to comport oneself within it need not be—indeed largely are not—conscious. To recognize beliefs as textual may be to begin thinking of them as mediated, as conveyed by some conditioned means, and for this reason texts that are most important for us may not be recognized as texts. They can be concealed by the world and the comportment that they provide and shape. However, it is not necessary that a text's role evaporates once the text becomes conscious. The conscious recognition of scripture and belief gradually recedes under the pressure of ongoing activities and experiences. However, it often does occur that scripture and belief are weakened when people are made conscious of them. This is both because awareness of a belief usually carries with it awareness that the belief comes from some particular and conditioned location and because some other belief has come into play without revealing either its mediated status or its nature as a belief. Students "lose their faith" when they go to college not only because they are made aware of their beliefs as mediated to them by texts but also because they are exposed to other beliefs promulgated as unmediated and as not beliefs.

Also, scriptures are not conclusions sedimented out of experience. It could as much be said that one has certain experiences because of beliefs as that one has certain beliefs because of experiences. However, given the scriptures of our culture, it is powerful rhetorically to refer to the basis of our beliefs, when called to do so, as experience. But it means no more to say that I experience things as I do because of my scripture than that I take things to be as they are because I experience them so to be. My beliefs cannot be separated from my experiences; my scriptures cannot be separated from my world.

Since beliefs are largely unconscious and are not simply derived from experience, and since clearly, at least for most people, beliefs change, the question arises, how do they change? This is too complicated a question to address, because the factors that create change are too numerous and because the possibility of change cannot itself be divorced from beliefs about change. Moreover, it is difficult to distinguish change in belief from modification or refinement of belief or from simple exchange by which a person's present beliefs are inversions of former beliefs now rejected, as is so often true of atheistic beliefs. Finally, it is as much to be expected that a person will become more entrenched in beliefs when they become conscious as that the person will reject them. I would say that in our culture beliefs change primarily because of the lingering notion that to have them is to be unenlightened and that full enfranchisement in the culture is tied to dissolving them. Indeed, one of the regnant beliefs of our culture is not only that we operate without beliefs and scriptures but that we live without the assistance of culture, encounter reality directly, and see things as they really are. Unlike other peoples and people of former centuries, we live in *the* world and not in *a* world, in the world as it *actually* is. Consequently, people in academic culture tend not to exchange beliefs for other beliefs but to value incredulity, cynicism, and impatience with belief above all else and imagine themselves in a world devoid not only of belief but of the conditionings and determinations of a particular culture.

Having addressed the role of beliefs in providing a world and guiding us within it, and having identified the actual or potential textuality of those beliefs as the scriptures of a person, group, or institution, I can move on to raise the more specific question of the beliefs required for an adequate, workable world to appear. It is not beliefs in general but beliefs of a certain kind that give a person or a group a world and ways of acting in it. In my view, the beliefs that provide these things can be categorized into four kinds. As I enumerate these four, I neither begin with the most important of them nor suggest that they all are of equal importance for every person or every group. Which of the four will be more important than the others varies as much as does the content of the four kinds of beliefs.

One kind of beliefs required for an adequate world concerns temporality. A person cannot carry on wholly undecided about his or her relation to natural, social, and personal processes. First, there is the formal question which of these processes is the most important. For example, should personal processes, the development of one's own interests, displace or defer to social processes and developments? Another matter to be settled is whether any or all of these processes ought to be trusted and affirmed or distrusted and resisted. For example, should the social and political processes in which I find myself be resisted or affirmed? Finally, there are beliefs concerning that to which processes lead and that from which they arose. Is the course of history, for example, downward or upward? Are there reasons to long for the past or eagerly to await the future? These are only some of the potential uncertainties that may arise from temporality. While some of these matters can remain undecided, a person, group, or institution has an adequate world and can carry on only if at least some beliefs in response to these uncertainties are in place.

The second set of beliefs required for an adequate, ongoing world concerns other people. A person, on getting up in the morning, also is at least partially prepared, without having to construct or be conscious of that preparation, to encounter other people. Beliefs are responses to such uncertainties as whether other people are basically good and trustworthy or bad and unreliable, whether they are fixed or changeable, whether they should be treated primarily as individuals or as members of some group, or whether they possess something of value. Beliefs about other persons can often be identified with prejudice and other forms of representation that allow a person or group to categorize large numbers of people in advance. The tenacity of prejudice, while related to other interests, especially political and economic, is difficult to separate entirely from the beliefs required of a person, group, or institution if an adequate world is to be in place. In any event, a person does not begin to act in his or her world without some set of beliefs about what people are like. The sense of other people and of the relations of a person, group, or institution to others forms a web of beliefs that cannot be open to total revision every day.

The third set of uncertainties that needs to be settled, at least partially, before an adequate world is in place concerns the borders that mark the jurisdictions and limits of a person, group, or institution, what possibilities these borders open or close, what negative or positive force these borders actually or potentially exert, and if and how what lies beyond them is significant. The borders of a world are both ontological and social, are both projected by and imposed on a particular world, and create conditions both positively and negatively related to the interests, needs, and potentials of that world. Beliefs identify these borders implicitly or explicitly and determine the kind of relations that exist between them and a person, group, or institution. In order to have a world, some understanding must be in place regarding what is possible, what can be expected, or what is allowed, both in terms of natural considerations and in terms derived from social, political, economic, and other such factors. All worlds are circumscribed, and the status, force, and permeability of those borders are matters of belief inscribed in particular scriptures.

The final set of beliefs that goes into the construction of an adequate world concerns the norms and values that determine judgments and selections. At least some of the following questions need to be answered before a person's day can begin: What is and what is not worth noticing or spending time on? How are people and their actions to be evaluated? How are the meaning and value of my actions to be judged? Such questions concerning selection and evaluation are crucial to waking up to or entering an adequate world. Choices and judgments will have to be made, and many of these, as well as the norms and procedures for making them, are matters settled before the choices or judgments arise.

It is not possible and, here, not necessary to give a full account of the process by which these four distinguishable but interrelated sets of beliefs come to be in place and allow an adequate world for a person or group to be constituted. However, it would be a mistake to think that these beliefs are acquired individually or separately. A person or a group acquires and is supported by a nest of beliefs, and because beliefs are related to one another, changes in one belief will affect the others. Explaining how beliefs are related to and affect one another, like explaining how beliefs arise and how they change, lies, by virtue of complexity, beyond the confines of this study.

These four kinds of beliefs can be textually identified because they and their relations to one another are borne by language. The most rudimentary and at the same time the clearest way in which the beliefs of a person or a group are made available is in and by language because utterances carry with them, by virtue of their subjects, predicates, situations, and voices, beliefs of all four kinds.

We are largely unaware that an utterance arises from and embodies beliefs, because with and through utterances we act in, presuppose, reconfirm, and challenge our world(s); beliefs are interwoven with the numerous occasions and goals in and for which we use language. However, we may become more aware of beliefs—or they may more easily be identified—in some forms of language use than in others. A narrative often allows the beliefs that are concealed in other language uses to appear more clearly. Narrative discourses to some degree step aside from nonnarrative discourses and require a different kind of attention. This is not to say that narrative discourses are not instrumental; they are, but they stand out at least somewhat from nonnarrative discourses and allow a kind of space to open up in which beliefs may become more noticeable. Nor is this to say that narrative is always the fullest and clearest way by which the beliefs borne in and by language come to attention, since other utterances—declarations, epithets, and cries of distress, for example—can be highly recognizable sites for the exposure of beliefs. It is simply to say that narratives hold an extraordinary potential for elaborating any or all of these four kinds of belief and for adumbrating or delineating the kind of worlds effected by beliefs.

Narratives hold this potential because the constitutive languages of narrative discourse evoke and address the four sets of uncertainties requiring beliefs. Constitutive of narrative discourse are languages of plot (temporal processes), character (other people), atmosphere (ontological and social conditions), and tone (evaluations, relations, and attitudes). It is not as though these four "languages" antedate narrative discourse, so that narratives are hybrids derived from a more original linguistic situation. Narratives are as basic to discourse as are nonnarrative utterances, and the beliefs incorporated by a narrative also are operative in the nonnarrative discourses of a person, group, or institution.

Although the many functions of narrative discourse—to convey information, to illustrate a point, to be funny, and so forth—distract attention from the beliefs that the languages of narrative carry, one important function of narrative discourse, to allow a world to be confirmed or interrogated, does not. Given this function, it should not be surprising that the major matters of traditions, including the recognized scriptures of peoples, have a primarily narrative form. While I would not want to say that narrative is required for the formation of an adequate world and indispensable for the scripture of a person, group, or institution, I would say that there exists an extraordinary relation between narratives and the worlds fashioned from beliefs that people live by and embody.

It remains, finally, only to point out that one of the reasons for the powerful role played by the Bible as the scriptures of many, differing people over so much time is its primarily narrative character. While there are numerous other kinds of discourses in the Bible, its most characteristic discourses are narratives. Moreover, the narratives of the Bible can be classified in terms of the preeminence gained by each of the four languages of narrative, so that biblical narratives seem to turn now to one and now to another of these four crucial areas of interest and uncertainty. Finally, it can be pointed out that God appears in various biblical narratives at each of the four points or in each of the four languages by which narratives are constituted. The reason for this now becomes available. God appears at all four points because each of them is both crucial to the provision of a world and associated with uncertainty. The combination of indispensable and uncertain makes each of the languages of narrative a ready point of connection or interaction between a human world and the transcendent.

The function of a person's or group's scriptures, then, is to articulate the beliefs that go into the construction of a world. Whatever it is that serves as the source, bearer, or validation of beliefs of the four kinds I have mentioned constitutes the scripture of a person, group, or institution. This need not always be a text in the normal sense of that word. A person may refer to an experience or what that person claims to be fact. But, of course, that reference is, as I have already said, textual.

III

Having looked, however briefly, at "scripture" both externally, as a category in textual and cultural theory that indicates location on the textual field, and internally, as providing the kinds of beliefs that constitute and sustain a world, I now consider a related but separable topic, namely, the practice of reading a text as scripture. What happens when we turn attention to our scriptures as something to be read? And what would it be like to read a text as scripture? The answer eludes us because this kind of reading has largely been displaced and marginalized in and by modern and postmodern cultures and no longer is something we are likely to do. It also eludes us because to read in this way has disconcerting consequences. As long as we do not read our scriptures as texts or texts as scriptures our locations and worlds can remain incontestable, taken for granted, or naturalized. But when we engage in such reading, we recognize that our locations are partial and our worlds are built on uncertainties. Understandably, we avoid such disconfirmations of adequacy and stability, and such avoidance is characteristic of our culture— in its religious as well as in its nonreligious segments, I would add. Indeed, if the word "secular" is to be used to describe our culture—and because of the specific theological interests it carries I otherwise do not use the word—it designates a culture that has lost its desire and capacity to read scripture. Why should anyone want to read scripture, when to read scripture is first of all to allow one's location and world to be disconfirmed and destabilized?

The search for an answer begins with a premodern, Calvin. This starting point is determined not by theology or ecclesiology but by history and culture. Calvin developed the fullest and most explicit doctrine of Scripture in the premodern period, and two aspects of that doctrine recommend it as a starting point. First, his doctrine of Scripture is primarily a doctrine of *reading* rather than a doctrine of the text. Indeed, I argue that Calvin's whole theology arises from and protects the theory of reading that underlies his doctrine of Scripture. Second, Calvin's theory of reading is not so much an invention as it is a combination of various strands that were available to him in the late medieval and Renaissance worlds. This means that his doctrine of the reading of Scripture is not so much the product and possession of a particular person and group but represents a site where a number of influences came, or were brought, together. This fact, it seems to me, accounts in part for the very great influence that Calvin's theory of reading had on the post-Reformation period.

In the second chapter, I suggest that beginning in the sixteenth century and throughout the modern period the principal residence of the kind of reading implied by Calvin's doctrine of Scripture shifted from the Bible to nature, then history, and, still later, to literature. Indeed, I take this shift to be crucial to the kind of culture produced by and characteristic of modernity. Initially, the practice of reading nature, then history, and finally literature as scripture was taken up and defended as warranted by the Bible. This warrant was derived primarily from biblical wisdom literature, texts that direct attention outward toward the three principal preoccupations of modernity, namely, the natural context of human life, human society and history, and spiritual ideals, enshrined in specially designated works of literature, toward which human beings should strive. Since the warrants for reading nature, history, and literature as scripture were derived from wisdom literature, modernity should be understood as enfolded by a sapiential religious system. The textual sources of this system, namely, biblical wisdom, were eclipsed because a second shift occurred, one by which the reading of nature, history, and literature as scripture was exchanged for the practice of reading the Bible as scripture. This shift finally produced a situation in which it was no longer generally recognized that reading nature, history, and literature had anything to do with reading the Bible or that the authority of nature, history, and literature had anything to do with a particular kind of reading practice, one derived from reading a text as scripture.

By severance from textual warrants and by the loss of understanding of what it means to read a text as scripture, the role of nature, history, and literature as sites for reading scripture could not be sustained; postmodernism primarily is a recognition and enactment of this severance and loss. Postmodernity is a cultural situation in which it is supposed that there are no scriptures and that nothing need, should, or could be read as though it were scripture. While postmodernism is a culture in reaction to the modern repression of textuality, it reinstates the textuality of culture without recovering or reconstituting the cultural practice of reading texts as scripture. Postmodernist theories of reading primarily accomplish for the reader of literature what already had been accomplished for the readers of history and, earlier, for the readers of nature, namely, to turn reading into processes of use, appropriation, and political advantage. The metaphors of economic exchange and political force, central to such theories, expose a situation that, like modernist assumptions it displaced, is taken as nontextual and not open to radical critique. But postmodernism is not a single or simple culture; important differences have emerged. Consequently, the chapter on postmodernism posits three stages or phases. It is hoped that this metaphor of progression will suggest both the continuity and the discontinuity that exist not only between these stages and their representatives but also between the third chapter and what follows it.

In the fourth chapter I turn to the works of Maurice Blanchot and Julia Kristeva as offering theories in which it is possible faintly to see what it might mean to read a text as though it were scripture. I treat them as continuous with the line projected by the previous chapter on postmodernism but also as separable in their implicit reformulation of what might now again be possible, namely, reading a text as scripture. I do not argue that they are premodernists or that, by having some similarities to Calvin, they reveal Calvin to be postmodernist before his time. I simply note, without minimizing the differences between them, some common aspects, especially in regard to what I call the centripetal aspect of reading in Calvin's theory.

In the Conclusion, I address the question whether it would be possible to read the Bible today as though it were scripture, to read it, that is, in ways that Blanchot and Kristeva suggest. This is not so arbitrary a question as at first it may sound, since Blanchot and Kristeva punctuate and illustrate their theories with references to biblical material, especially to biblical narratives.

Indeed, I contend that the reasons why similarities can be drawn between Calvin and Blanchot and Kristeva, so vastly different from one another as in other ways they are, is that they all use biblical paradigms and patterns for developing what it means to read a text. I will suggest, at the appropriate time, that the Bible can be read as primarily directing what it would and should be like to read it, that its stories are about, among other things, how they should be read. This allows a third tie to be drawn between the textual or cultural category of scripture and biblical texts. Not only are biblical texts ready candidates for the role of scripture by virtue of their ability to grant locations to diverse people and, by the use of narrative discourses, to call attention to the languages that constitute and challenge a world, but they also have the potential to instruct the reader in how they should be read. The principal "message" of the Bible for our culture is how to read a text as though it were scripture.

CHAPTER ONE

THE THEORY OF READING IN CALVIN'S DOCTRINE OF SCRIPTURE

I begin this study in the practice of reading a text as scripture with the sixteenth century, particularly with the work of John Calvin. I do so because Calvin developed the fullest (one is tempted to say the only) doctrine of Scripture in the Reformation.[1] More important, his doctrine deals not so much with the nature of biblical texts or with their origins as with *reading* them. Finally, the theory of reading embedded in his doctrine of Scripture is not idiosyncratic; rather, it is drawn from sources readily available to him and generally known to his readers. Consequently, choosing Calvin as a place to begin is not a move of exclusion and isolation, for Calvin can be seen as a site where a number of cultural assumptions, interests, and practices converge.

It is tempting to defend using the sixteenth century as the starting point of a narrative that ends in our own time by listing similarities between pre- and postmodernist cultures, but I am more impressed by the differences and distances between our culture and Calvin's than by similarities and continuities between them. True, like our own, Calvin's time was one of disenchantment with the adequacy of philosophical and theological systems;[2] also like our own, it was a time when institutions and their practices and powers were subjected to critique. In ways similar to our own, intellectual activity was inseparable from political goals and consequences. And, like our own, Calvin's culture was fragmented and transitional, "a peculiarly troubled age."[3] But such similarities, however helpful they may be for understanding Calvin, do not account for his theory of reading, which is derived more from traditional doctrines and practices than from such cultural currents as these. In addition, despite similarities, Calvin's culture differs from our own in three ways relevant to this study. First, Calvin could assume a cultural "Platonism," that is, a general orientation to the transcendent that not only cannot now be assumed but also has been the object of philosophical attack in our own time at least since Nietzsche.[4] Second, the Bible and theological and devotional works dependent on it were dominant texts not only among clergy and the educated but also increasingly, in Calvin's day, among more ordinary people. Finally, reading these texts was closely tied to religious discipline and devotion, and Calvin could assume a culture in which reading the Bible was a specific and developed religious practice.[5] While I would not want to underestimate the importance of Biblical texts and the reading of them for modern and postmodern Western culture, and while I do not discount the similarities between our culture and Calvin's, his culture, by means of traditional disciplines and a generally accepted philosophical outlook, supported the practice of reading Scripture as our own culture does not. Consequently, there is no possibility simply of transporting or even translating this topic from his culture to our own. Recovery will also require reconstruction.

However, within this mix of similarities and differences between Calvin's culture and our own, one matter of continuity I want to maintain. It is the cultural placement and effects of his theory of reading Scripture. The temptation today would be to design a theory of reading scripture in and for a specific confessional community, since our culture seems such infertile ground for transplanting this premodern practice. But this is not the move taken in this study, because the theory and practice embedded in Calvin's doctrine of Scripture were important not only for Calvin's culture and for the premodern period generally but also for modernity. Indeed, I argue that the lacks and problems of postmodernism must be seen in relation to the loss of reading scripture because this loss has resulted in inadequate cultural or textual theories and practices. Moreover, it would be a mistake, if not an illusion, to think that a community within the culture could be isolated from its major currents, could have a culture entirely its own, or could re-create a premodern culture in defiance of its context. Such notions of separation or transcendence, while theologically fashionable and attractive, are not viable. For these reasons, I intend first of all to incorporate into textual and cultural theory the practice of reading scripture, with the realization that this decision, while it will open some doors, will close others.

To get at Calvin's theory of reading we must first step backward to assess, however briefly, practices of reading Scripture that Calvin assumed as background and material. We can then turn to the theory itself, which, as we shall see, is largely a reconstruction and new application of assumptions and practices he took over from his own and preceding times. Finally, we should look at the status of Calvin's doctrine of reading Scripture in his theological work more generally considered.

I

It is important to notice, when turning to Calvin's doctrine of reading Scripture, that he extends the act of reading in ways that we generally do not. For example, he does not limit reading to the eyes. Possibly because reading was often audible, he as often refers to reading as a way of hearing as of seeing. Indeed, frequently when Calvin refers to the hearing of the Word he has reading Scripture in mind. This close identification of reading and hearing is also supported by the relation that exists for Calvin between reading Scripture and hearing preaching. Calvin's own preaching was determined by the progression of the biblical texts, and the structure and content of a particular sermon was determined by reading the text.[6] Calvin's theory of reading, then, often directs a person to read with an attitude appropriate to hearing, that is, to read with receptivity or passivity. While Calvin also liked visual metaphors for reading, such as his famous figure that compares reading Scripture to donning spectacles that clear up blurry eyesight,[7] aural language for reading is very important to him. His use of it does not suggest, however, that preaching should subsume reading, as may be appropriate with Luther; with Calvin, reading Scripture is primary. "Hearing" means reading even when it refers to preaching, because the preaching that Calvin has in mind and practiced is determined by and remains very close to the reading of Scripture.

In addition to relating reading to hearing, Calvin relates reading to eating. This has its biblical warrant in passages that explicitly refer to the eating of texts (Jeremiah, Ezekiel, and Revelation). A sense of reading as an act of ingestion, of allowing the text to become a part of oneself and of taking the words as nourishment, accounts for the close relation that exists for Calvin between reading Scripture and receiving the Sacrament. Indeed, the "as if" language that Calvin uses for the reading of Scripture he also uses for receiving Christ in the Sacrament. This close relation of the two acts allows Calvin to make a crucial exchange: he gives to reading

Scripture the centrality that the medieval church had given to receiving the Sacrament.

Calvin, however, not only relates reading to hearing and eating, he also extends the act of reading outward beyond written texts to nature and history. As the language of hearing and eating internalizes the act of reading, so reading nature and events extends textuality and reading outward indefinitely and suggests the kind of relevance that reading Scripture had to understanding the larger world. This extension of reading accounts for Calvin's placing his doctrine of Scripture in the *Institutes* in the context of a general discussion of the relation of people to events and things around them and the knowledge of God that they could derive from reading the texts of nature and history.

When Calvin situates reading Scripture in relation to the internalizing acts of hearing and eating and to the externalizing act of reading nature and history, he deals simply with priorities—reading Scripture is primary, on the one side, to preaching and sacraments and, on the other, to reading nature and history. But on another matter, the relation of reading Scripture to reading religious and ecclesiastical art, Calvin is more radical. At the fountainhead of this topic are the two letters that Pope Gregory the Great sent to Serenus of Marseilles, who had begun destroying works of religious art. Gregory articulated the theory not only that paintings should be read but that religious art, especially wall paintings in churches, constituted a scripture for the illiterate. With these letters, written in 599 and 600, as background, the medieval church debated this matter, particularly because it was not clear what Gregory had in mind. Indeed, it is still not clear to scholars whether he meant that uneducated people could gain from paintings knowledge they previously did not have or that paintings could merely clarify, intensify, or apply to life previously and differently acquired knowledge.[8] Calvin's attack on the practice of reading art as scripture, while not confined to the terms of that debate, is affected by them.[9] The principal religious point for Calvin arises from his visible/invisible distinction; depictions of the invisible in religious art allowed its readers direct access to spiritual things, while reading the Bible did not. As important for him is the political point: reading pictures kept the Bible out of the hands of ordinary people and deprived their reading of the authority it should have. What developed from Gregory's teaching was a political as well as a cultural distinction, one both between those who could read Latin and those who, because they could not, had to settle for reading pictures and between clergy and laity. Calvin engaged an important political issue when he democratized the reading of Scripture. While it may be too much to say that Calvin attacks reading paintings because it confined reading the Bible to clerical and elite privilege, it certainly can be said that his insistence on the primacy of reading the Bible for every Christian's life carried a significant social and even political consequence.[10] His doctrine of reading Scripture put great power in the hands of ordinary people, and this political issue is inseparable from the theological.

The sources upon which Calvin drew for the theory of reading embedded in his doctrine of Scripture included, first and foremost, the monastic practice of *lectio divina*. This major discipline, which follows the direction of Saint Benedict, was focused on the reading of biblical texts.[11] As Jean Leclercq points out, it was a way of reading intended to allow the texts to have maximum effect on the reader, even to be inscribed on the reader's body. The language used for this act is that of eating. The text is taken as though by mouth, and the recipient ruminates on it; "the vocabulary is borrowed from eating, from digestion, and from the particular form of digestion belonging to ruminants," says Leclercq.[12] By reading, one receives the text with the *palatum cordis*.[13] Reading, then, is not reducible to communicating information. Reading is an act of "communion with God, first of all with words, concepts and images and then, ideally without them."[14] *Lectio* is inseparable from *meditatio*, from prayer and contemplation. In my opinion Calvin could not have accomplished what he did with his doctrine of reading Scripture if it were not for the tradition of *lectio divina*. By his doctrine of Scripture, he took this practice out of its monastic setting and inserted it into the life of every Christian.

A second source for Calvin's doctrine of reading Scripture is the new learning that pervaded the atmosphere of Paris during his formative years there.[15] He was influenced by currents of thought that combined what could be called humanism with a theological Augustinianism that avoided the Pelagian anthropology usually associated with the *via moderna*.[16] In this milieu, reading took on a particular kind of power and significance.

For one thing, reading held a reforming and transforming theological and institutional potential. As Alister McGrath puts it, "The rise of humanistic textual and linguistic techniques showed up the alarming discrepancies between the [Latin] Vulgate and the texts it was supposed to translate— and thus opened the way to doctrinal reformation."[17] The ability to read biblical texts in original languages gave to readers not only the sense that they could bypass the mediation provided by medieval commentaries and read the texts directly but also the awareness that at least some medieval beliefs, practices, structures, and authorities were based on or supported by mistranslations of the Hebrew and Greek texts. Calvin notes mistranslations in the Latin Vulgate, and knowledge of ancient languages gave him and others a powerful weapon to subvert and attack the authority of the Roman Church and its theology and practices over Scripture.[18] It became possible to read the Church and its doctrines in the light of Scripture rather than to read Scripture in the light of the Church and doctrine. This is crucial to Calvin's reversal of the priorities of theology or of institution and text. In his own ecclesiology, the church, in its practices and beliefs, is derived from and needs to be judged in relation to the reading of Scripture.

In addition, placing Scripture over, rather than under, the church gave to Calvin a critical tool by which the simple supplanted the power and privilege of the complicated and elaborated.[19] A repeated theme in Calvin's critical discussion of the Roman Church is not only how complex it had become in its ceremonies and interpretations of Scripture but also how much value and authority had become associated with such elaborations. Calvin's critique of the tradition is not based on a rejection of the value of history in general but of a particular history, one that had turned what was simple, direct, and available to ordinary people into something complex and mediated to ordinary people by a few. Consequently, a political consequence of reading Scripture also arose from the *via moderna*. Now the simplest Christian as reader of Scripture potentially held as much authority as bishops and their institutional and doctrinal fortifications. Calvin's many attacks on the power of the Roman Church in relation to the value of Christian freedom can be seen as a defense of the potential authority given to every Christian by virtue of reading Scripture.

Calvin was not alone among the new humanists in his emphasis on reading as the right and obligation of free Christians. One can see it also in Erasmus.[20] In his *Enchiridion* Erasmus, using the language of the *lectio divina*, urges the Christian to meditate on Scripture day and night. One should come to the reading of Scripture as to a meal, "with washed hands, that is with the greatest purity of mind." Erasmus also anticipates Calvin's famous doctrine of divine accommodation when, continuing his eating metaphors for reading, he writes, "Divine wisdom speaks to us in baby-talk and like a living mother accommodates its words to our state of infancy. It offers milk to tiny infants in Christ, and herbs to the sick."[21] It would be difficult to overstress how important reading Scripture was in the context of the new learning in which Calvin was educated; reading Scripture was a highly charged and focused religious, cultural, and political act.

A third influence on Calvin's theory of reading was the hermeneutical reforms of Nicholas of Lyra (Normandy), who taught in Paris during the first half of the fourteenth century. In constant contact with Jewish scholars, thought by some himself to have had Jewish parentage, and particularly indebted to Rabbi Shelomoh ben Yitshaq of Troyes (1040–1105), Nicholas knew the Hebrew language well, deplored the state of Christian biblical scholarship, and advocated the plain meaning of the texts. His *Postilla Litteralis* was widely referred to and was the first printed biblical commentary (1471–72). It provided a mode of biblical reading important to the Reformers, and Calvin pits it against ultramontane interpretations of Scripture that he never tires of referring to as willful and fanciful.[22]

The plain sense of the text, the new learning, the *lectio divina*, the debates on the reading of paintings, and the relation of reading both to hearing and eating and to nature and history provided Calvin the context and the materials in and by which he constructed his doctrine of reading Scripture. Primarily what he did, as I have already suggested, was to take practices and terms at hand and to make new combinations and applications of them. His crucial acts were to move the practice of reading Scripture from the monastery and from clerical circles to all Christians, to exchange the centrality of receiving the sacraments for the centrality of reading Scripture, and to make the reading of Scripture the determining and defining practice of Christian life.

II

The discursive situation in which Calvin deploys his doctrine of reading Scripture is defined primarily by Roman and Anabaptist alternatives that he considers as standing on either side of him. In contrast to the Roman position, which subjects the text to the institution, Calvin subordinates the institution to the text. The church is not the source of and does not have authority over Scripture; Scripture is the source of and has authority over the church. "But a most pernicious error widely prevails that Scripture has only so much weight as is conceded to it by the consent of the church. As if the eternal and inviolable truth of God depended upon the decision of men!" He is equally opposed to spiritualists, on the other side, who elevate religious experience over Scripture and claim that the Holy Spirit is revealed to people apart from reading Scripture. "For of late, certain giddy men have arisen who, with great haughtiness exalting the teaching office of the Spirit, despise all reading and laugh at the simplicity of those who, as they express it, still follow the dead and killing letter."[23] In response to these alternatives— the primacy of the church and the primacy of unmediated experience of the Holy Spirit—Calvin makes reading Scripture central. Apart from it, people have no relation with or saving knowledge of God.

A second discursive context of Calvin's theory of reading is that of classical learning and contemporary interest in classical rhetoric and style. Calvin insists that it is not the qualities of the text that give the Bible its central and authoritative position; indeed, Calvin was well aware that in many respects the Bible did not commend itself as edifying or impressive in content or in style, and he takes a kind of Pauline delight in biblical crudeness, as though the power of the Holy Spirit is made clearer when the rhetorical weakness of the texts, in comparison to classical examples, is recognized. "For it was also not without God's extraordinary providence that the sublime mysteries of the Kingdom of Heaven came to be expressed largely in mean and lowly words, lest, if they had been adorned with most shining eloquence, the impious would scoffingly have claimed that its power is in the realm of eloquence alone." Following Erasmus, Calvin augments his interpretation of the often crude qualities of the texts by adding to this Pauline explanation the thought that in these texts God is accommodated to human understandings. This accommodation readers must accept. "For who even of slight intelligence does not understand that, as nurses commonly do with infants, God is wont in a measure to 'lisp' in speaking to us? Thus such forms of speaking do not so much express clearly what God is like as accommodate the knowledge of him to our slight capacity. To do this he must descend far beneath his loftiness."[24] Taken together, these two points have important consequences. The first allows Calvin to emphasize that the power of reading cannot be located in the text itself. The second means that knowledge of God cannot be separate from reading the texts. For Calvin, there is no saving knowledge of God, no experience of the Holy Spirit, and no relation to Christ apart from the primary act of reading Scripture.[25]

Power is at the core of Calvin's theory of reading. While one reads the texts for knowledge and meaning, they are secondary to Scripture's power.[26] Calvin attributes to the power of the texts their ability not only to survive but to play influential roles in diverse cultures. Indeed, Calvin uses some terms traditionally applied to the endurance and ubiquity of the church to celebrate the power of the Scriptures. But it is only in reading Scripture that its power can fully and beneficially be experienced. "Then, in spite of yourself, so deeply will it affect you, so penetrate your heart, so fix itself in your very marrow, that, compared with its deep impression, such vigor as orators and philosophers have will nearly vanish."[27] I emphasize that the power of a text is a dominant consideration for Calvin because we almost exclusively think of reading as receiving information or as deciphering meaning. Power for Calvin is both personal, the power to penetrate the reader's heart, and cultural, the power of the text to endure and to influence diverse cultures.

A third discursive situation for Calvin's doctrine of reading Scripture is interest in and reflection on nature and history. This is an important and difficult matter, for it would appear that for Calvin the primacy of Scripture, the need of the Christian to forsake all other ways of knowing or being in relation to God for this one, suggests that reading Scripture forms a kind of island in a threatening sea of ignorance or distortion regarding knowledge of God. While I insist that for Calvin the reading of Scripture is absolutely central, I do not mean that for him Creation and history were evil and devoid of knowledge of God. Indeed, he says much to the contrary. Calvin had a high view of Creation and believed that enough knowledge of God was present there to render people without excuse who did not recognize in it the power and grace of God. Calvin also had a high regard for the civic order and cultural accomplishments of the ancient world, and he believed that the power of God was active in such history. The question is how Calvin had it both ways, a concentrated doctrine of the unique role of Scripture and a strong doctrine of Creation and Providence. The clue to a resolution of this ambiguity in his work is Calvin's assumption that whatever is good comes from God.[28] This means that the good that is in Creation or in human accomplishments is not possessed by them but is a good that is granted to them by God's power and grace. The process of reading Scripture, then, is first of all marked by divestment, by the elimination of any claims the reader might make that the reader brings something of use, some good, humanly or naturally possessed, that will contribute to the consequences of reading. And when nature or history, otherwise locations of imparted divine goodness, become distractions from, obstacles to, or substitutes or directives for reading Scripture, they became evil. While for Calvin there is much that is good in the world, this goodness is not the possession of things or people. In order to recognize this, a person has to be divested of any notion that he or she comes to the reading of Scripture with a goodness that is a possession.[29]

Crucial to this reading of Scripture, according to Calvin's doctrine, is a distinction between two moments in reading. This distinction is implied or assumed more than it is articulated and defended. Let us call the distinguishable but not separate moments of reading "centripetal" and "centrifugal."

By centripetal reading I mean a focusing and minimalizing process by which the reader attends to two bits of crucial knowledge. This act of concentration and the knowledge that draws and warrants it have life-changing consequences. Saving knowledge and the process of divestment and concentration are related, but the reading does not cause the knowledge; the reader realizes, after reading, that the knowledge caused the reading. Saving knowledge penetrates the heart of the reader and produces in the reader's life a change of direction. It has these effects because it is imparted to the reader's life by power, and the reader recognizes that it would not have been received unless the reader's heart had been prepared and this knowledge imparted to it. When Calvin implies this act, which I am calling centripetal reading, he draws on all three of his major sources but most directly on the practice of *lectio divina* as it comes to him primarily in and through the work of Saint Bernard.[30]

The content of the knowledge received in and through centripetal reading is this: the name of the one who has created everything and knowledge that the one who has created everything also redeems.[31] This knowledge is not otherwise available. Calvin could assume that people believed in and had knowledge of God, but only in and by reading Scripture are these two bits of knowledge granted to readers by the power of the Holy Spirit. This knowledge, inseparable from centripetal reading, makes all the difference. Indeed, there is a contrary relation between this knowledge and the knowledge of God that one has from observations and experiences of Creation and history, because this knowledge is deeply relational and personal. The reader learns God's name and recognizes that the process of divestment in reading was part of the reader's redemption, being freed, that is, from bondage to this world and from identity with a sinful self.

Since there is a contrary relation between the world and self that the reader brings to reading and the saving knowledge that comes in and through centripetal reading, the act of reading Scripture involves and requires above all divestment and dislocation. A negative relation arises between the reader's world and self and the saving knowledge of God available only in and by reading Scripture, because the saving knowledge of God is not added to otherwise acquired knowledge of God but, rather, other knowledge of God needs now to be reconstituted in the light of knowledge granted in and through centripetal reading. And this displacement and reconstitution is a part of reading Scripture every time it occurs. The act of reading centripetally is inseparable from a willingness to let go of everything else, including the self, and to count all that otherwise might be thought of as good as a potential obstacle, substitute, or diversion.

It is fair to say that the two theologians in the tradition that have the greatest impact on Calvin and consequences for his theology are Saint Augustine and Saint Bernard.[32] Their influence can also be felt in his doctrine of the reading of Scripture.[33] From Augustine he receives, of course, a high regard for reading Scripture, but, even more important, he receives from Augustine an epistemology that recognizes saving knowledge as divinely imparted. From Saint Bernard comes not only the *lectio divina* but the general sense of discipline that one finds clearly elaborated by Saint Bernard in his meditation on and prescription of the states of humility.[34]

For Saint Bernard, the path to truth begins with humility, and humility is a painfully won recognition, discovered by disciplined self-scrutiny, of personal unworthiness. The effect of this scrutiny is that one feels alienated from others because of unworthiness. When a person, because of sin, feels most alienated, most dissociated from others and from God, the person can recognize what it means to be human, that is, to be sinful, and what God is like, namely, gracious. In contrast, the steps of pride lead one from a sense of personal worth to a sense of disregard for others and of autonomy before God.

I sketch Saint Bernard's discipline of divestment and concentration and the knowledge of self and God to which it is hoped such a discipline would lead not in order to say that Calvin's doctrine of reading Scripture follows it step by step. But this sort of practice was very much a part both of Calvin's religious understanding and of his cultural context, since the works of both Saint Augustine and Saint Bernard were best-sellers during the rising market of printed books in the first half of the sixteenth century.[35] This helps to explain why Calvin does not go into greater detail about what I am calling centripetal reading. The general understanding of religious discipline suggested above and the particular tradition of the *lectio divina* were widely recognizable and made greater detailing of this component of the act of reading unnecessary. Rather, what Calvin does primarily is to take these traditions and apply them to the reading of Scripture as absolutely central and crucial to the life of each Christian.

For Calvin, the reader does not produce the consequences of centripetal reading; those consequences are effected by the Holy Spirit. What the reader *can* do is to read "as if" in Scripture the living Word of God is to be heard.[36] The "sicut" construction in his doctrine of reading Scripture, which Calvin provides also for receiving the sacraments, marks the limit, the extent, to which human effort contributes to the results of centripetal reading. There is no guarantee in the reader's hand that can be cashed in at the end of reading.

While the fruits of centripetal reading are absolutely crucial for Calvin, he does not end here. His theory of reading Scripture also contains a centrifugal moment, one that moves from saving knowledge outward not only to the whole of Scripture but to the relation of Scripture to the whole of life.

It is important to notice, in contrast to other Reformers, particularly to Luther, that the two aspects, or moments, in the reading of Scripture are not distinguished on the basis of differing texts. That is, Calvin does not relate centripetal reading to one part of the Bible, say, to the New Testament, and centrifugal reading to the rest, say, to the Old. While he privileges centripetal over centrifugal reading, he does not so readily or clearly privilege some biblical texts over others. Although the knowledge of who God is and that God is one who saves as well as one who creates is clearer in some parts of the Bible than in others, it is available anywhere and everywhere, as far as Calvin is concerned.

Centrifugal reading is not "upward," in the sense advanced by the spiritualist contemporaries to whom Calvin often refers or by such theologians in the tradition as Origen. Calvin is opposed to such extensions and elaborations as fanciful and willful. Rather than upward, Calvin wants extensions in the reading of Scripture to be outward, to form as wide and adequate a basis for life as possible. Calvin has confidence in the extensions made by Christians because they are based on, are the fruits of, saving knowledge. The Christian who reads in this outward way is one whose life has been radically altered in and through centripetal reading.

The emphasis on extension accounts for Calvin's quite remarkable approbation of the Old Testament.[37] True, the saving knowledge of God is clearer and more widely offered in the New Testament than in the Old, but it is also fully and adequately offered there. Israel is a true church and not an erroneous or deficient one, and the Law, while it finds its principal role in the diagnosis of sin, has a true, although subordinate and often obscured, role in teaching salvation. "The people [of Israel] was a figure of the Christian church; but it was itself the true Church; its condition was a sketch of our own; but as such it had even at the time the proper character of the Church."[38] Calvin wanted to affirm as much as possible the whole of the Bible and the integrity of its many parts in order to make it enabling and productive in all aspects of life. Once the basic bits of saving knowledge have been applied to a person's life, an event that unites all Christians by the work of the Holy Spirit, all of Scripture becomes profitable for a critique and restructuring of the church, the Christian life, and the civic order.

It may be helpful to distinguish Calvin's doctrine of the reading of Scripture from notions one encounters today in circles that claim loyalty to his work. For one thing, Calvin's doctrine of the reading of Scripture turns against the possibility of treating the Bible as an icon, an object identified as the presence of God in our world. Calvin militates against this notion not only in his emphasis on the "living words of God" as inseparable from the activity of the Holy Spirit but also in his attack, while developing his doctrine of reading Scripture, on statues and paintings and their uses within the Roman Church. Calvin's point in this discussion is not only the one I mentioned above, namely, an attack on preserving the reading of Scripture for a small, primarily clerical group of Christians, but also a point about idolatry. Central to the discussion is Calvin's distinction between the visible and the invisible and his conviction that people always want to but never should make the invisible visible. This is a point Calvin vigorously makes because of what he takes to be an irrepressible human need and desire to make idols.[39] Calvin is not opposed to all painting and all sculpture, but he insists that they should be of visible things and events. This is important for his constant attempt not to mistake things that are human for things that are divine. When visible things and events are depicted in art, we have a sense that people have done this work, that these depictions are, we could say, fictional. But when the invisible is depicted, we may lose a sense of the fictional character of the depiction, and it may be confused with the thing depicted. Calvin dwells on the lapse of the children of Israel into idolatry in the desert because it is paradigmatic for him of the human attempt to substitute a visible presence for the absence or invisibility of God. His reading of this as typical, even predictable and definitive, human behavior fuels his attacks on the sacramental theories and practices of the Roman Church. Consequently, any doctrine of Scripture that would end in viewing the Bible as the visible or tangible presence of God in our world would not only contradict Calvin's doctrine of the reading of Scripture but violate what is central to and determinative of his entire theology.

A second common understanding of the Bible that seems to have no basis in Calvin is that the Bible is a "witness" to the Word of God. This view suggests a separation between the letter and the spirit that Calvin rejects.

So, when commenting on Paul's statement that the letter kills and the spirit gives life, Calvin takes Paul to mean by "letter" the Law divorced from Holy Spirit or the Law used willfully or as an end in itself.[40] Calvin did not posit a gap between letter and spirit that such language as "the Bible is a witness to the Word of God" would suggest. Also, Calvin would not posit the Bible as a "witness" to God or Christ, because such a position would suggest that God or Christ are somehow known apart from reading Scripture. Calvin insists that people have no dealing with God or Christ apart from Scripture. Here is a typical statement: "[I]f we would know Christ, we must seek him in the Scriptures. Anyone who imagines Christ as he will, gets nothing but a mere blur. So, we must first hold that Christ is known rightly nowhere but in Scripture."[41] The identification of saving knowledge and reading Scripture is much closer than the language of "witness" suggests. Either a position that assumes the living words of God to be identical with the written page or a position that assumes a gap between them cannot be taken as consistent with Calvin.

III

Measuring the status of Calvin's doctrine of reading Scripture in the rest of his work requires a brief look at its consequences for his understanding of the church, theology, and the Christian life. I have already mentioned some consequences for his understanding of the church; in a word, Calvin reverses authorities, so that the church derives from reading Scripture and not reading Scripture from the church. In addition, the church is defined not in terms of its clergy but in terms of its people. Last, the church is not a physical institution but a community of Scripture readers. To be considered further are the consequences of Calvin's doctrine of reading Scripture for the unity of the church. Why does Calvin not consider the threat posed by his doctrine to the unity of the church sufficient reason for modifying or even abandoning it?

First of all, it should be said that for Calvin unity, like goodness, comes from God. This means that unity is not a human invention, and it means that unity is invisible. It should also be clear that for Calvin there is a basic unity among Christians because the saving knowledge of God granted in and through the centripetal reading of Scripture is imparted by the power of the Holy Spirit. Since this event is determinative and definitive of the life of the Christian, occurs, that is, not by the will of flesh but of the Spirit, then all Christians by definition are basically unified. This is the unity that counts most, that makes all the difference. Diversity and differences are relatively unimportant in comparison to it.

Differences arise from that aspect of the reading of Scripture that I have called centrifugal. Christians in various situations will draw diverse conclusions and apply them differently or in differing situations. It appears that Calvin minimized the extent and gravity of these differences.[42] He did so because he believed that centripetal reading, which unifies, would have a determining effect on centrifugal reading. Furthermore, since a saving knowledge of God does not arise without undermining assumptions of the inherent goodness and reliability of things human, centripetal reading would expose and counter all centrifugal readings that are self-serving, willful, or fanciful. But it is also probably true that Calvin too often took the text to be perspicuous and not to sponsor a variety of interpretations. He seems to be unprepared for difference and diversity as a major problem.

However, he does descry a second form or occasion of unity among readers of Scripture.[43] The Holy Spirit also operates within the community to bring about unity among Christians who at first may differ in their centrifugal readings of Scripture. Calvin admires the early councils of the church and the unity that arose out of sharp diversity of opinions.[44] Calvin seems to be confident that whatever unity there needs to be in centrifugal reading, if it is not assured by the definitive and determining consequences of the work of the Holy Spirit in centripetal reading, will be created by the work of the Holy Spirit in the deliberations of Christians among one another.[45]

Calvin was aware that differences and diversity would remain, and he often refers to differing thoughts and practices in many areas of Christian and church life. These do not strike one always as minor matters: the mode of administering the sacraments, for example, or Paul's prohibition against women's speaking in the church.[46] But by definition, Calvin takes such differences and diversity, since they have not been unified by the work of the Holy Spirit, to be matters of relative unimportance. One could put this differently: whatever stands as a matter of difference between Christians—as long as it is clear that these are Christians defined by centripetal reading and Christians who have, in the spirit of that reading, extended Scripture outward in a way that is not self-serving and who have not tried to advance themselves in their deliberations with other members of the church—is relatively unimportant or should be allowed to remain unresolved. What operates in such instances is the kind of spirit that Paul advocated to the Corinthian church regarding differences of practice and belief concerning the eating of meat dedicated to gods. What should operate is the honoring of Christian freedom and a stewardship of that freedom that makes a Christian's concern for the moral and spiritual well-being of the fellow Christian more important than the exercise of his or her own freedom.[47]

Difference, finally, is for Calvin not only a negative factor in the life of the church. It carries reforming potential, and the church is always in need of reform. Only by readings of Scripture that are to some degree in opposition to the current beliefs or practices of the church can reform occur.

The purpose of theology is to aid in the reading of Scripture. But it can neither substitute for reading Scripture nor control it. As John Leith contends, "Calvin's *Institutes* were not designed for the theologically elite [not an option for Calvin] but for the Christian *as a reader of Scripture*."[48] The idea that one reads Scripture in order to develop a theology that one then substitutes for or imposes on the reading of Scripture is antithetical to Calvin's doctrine. Theology does not determine the reading of Scripture, and reading Scripture does not harden into a doctrine of the text or of reading it. Theology, doctrine, and even dogma are always vulnerable to correction by reading Scripture.

It may even be possible to say that Calvin's characteristic theological emphases are elaborations and protections of the theory of reading that is so central for him. Such matters as the saving knowledge of God and its relation to knowledge of God otherwise derived, the need to denounce reliance on one's self or one's world and to count as nothing what one might be tempted to bring to the saving knowledge of God, the power of the Holy Spirit to prepare the heart for that knowledge and to impart it, and the doctrines of sin, repentance, and redemption—matters so important to him—are clarifications, amplifications, and protections of what it means to read Scripture as though there the living words of God were heard.[49] The doctrines for which Calvin is so well known—election, sin, grace, predestination, or the sovereignty of God—should be read first of all as prescriptive for the practice of reading Scripture rather than as descriptive of God, human beings, history, or nature.

Calvin does not treat Scripture as a kind of ladder by which one rises to a level where one is related to God without Scripture. If this is implied in monastic disciplines of *lectio divina*, then Calvin does not follow that practice to its conclusion. For Calvin, a person has always to do with God as God is accommodated to the reader in and by Scripture.[50] This does not mean that one's knowledge of and relation to God are confined to the moments when one reads Scripture but that that knowledge and relation, when they become more general, are always conditioned and corrected by the centripetal reading of Scripture. One moves out from centripetal reading back to the world and understands the world differently, understands and constructs it in terms of the saving knowledge of God, but one must also be prepared to release those applications and investments when centripetal reading is again taken up.

For Calvin, nothing is more crucial, more basic, or more determinative for the Christian life than the reading of Scripture. Everything else depends upon and follows from it, and if anything has standing in and for the Christian life, it derives from or is analogous to the reading of Scripture. It is the occasion when or the site where the basic, transforming event in a person's life occurs. The church is a company of readers, and preaching "borrows its status of Word of God from Scripture."[51]

Consequently, a Christian life based on reading is inescapably solitary, but Calvin's solitary reader is not comprehensible using understandings of privacy or of the individual current in our own culture. Calvin would have nothing to do with the privileged place we give to privacy or with either our ontology or ethic of the individual. He has no place for the autonomy or primacy of personal experience. Even such notions of the private, of personal experience, or of the individual that were available to him he attributes to willfulness and arrogance. For example, in his commentary on 2 Pet. 1:20, which speaks against private interpretation, Calvin takes "private" to mean not solitary but privately concocted and self-serving. The saving knowledge of God made available by the Holy Spirit in the process of reading is anything but "private" in our sense of individualistic. Calvin did not advocate private religion or the primacy of personal religious experience. The Holy Spirit that imparts saving knowledge to the heart of the solitary reader is the Holy Spirit that at the same time unites that reader with other Christians so constituted. Reading is solitary, a process, like dying, of divestment, but the saving knowledge of God is shared and is not a privileged possession of separate individuals.

Furthermore, the Christian, while solitary in centripetal reading and unified with other Christians by a saving knowledge of God, moves out of solitariness to the church and out of the church into the world in order to translate knowledge of God into concrete structures and actions. This outward direction is without bounds. What makes Calvinism so expandable or so suited for an expanding and diversifying world is this outward thrust.[52]

The Christian life, finally, is marked by a diligent application of Scripture to the whole of life. Scripture has consequences for and can be extended and applied to everything. The Christian, in some way like the Christian soldier in Erasmus, is loosed on the world in order to change it. The deployment and freedom of the Christian, the confidence placed in Christians and the Christian life, and the consequent openness and spread are contagious and dynamic. The doctrine of Scripture, while giving primacy to a minimalist, concentrated reading, moves out, by means of centrifugal reading, in the widest possible way, and it does so by means of the Christian life.

CHAPTER TWO

MODERNITY

*Reading Other Texts As Though They,
and Not the Bible, Were Scripture*

Calvin's theory of reading, as I have shown, is representative of his culture and not an exception or radical departure from it. This representative standing may account for the wide dissemination of his theory, a dissemination that increasingly separated this way of reading from the devotional and ecclesiastical contexts in which it arose. In this chapter I trace crucial reapplications of this theory and practice of reading to other texts and contexts and suggest their importance for the formation of modern culture. These other locations, in chronological order, are nature, history, and finally literature. Each of these three texts comes to be read as though it were scripture. At first each of the three is read as supplementary to the Bible, but then each becomes a competing and then a supplanting scripture. The narrative I propose is one that moves, then, not only from reading nature to reading history and then to reading literature as scripture but also from reading these other texts first as a practice warranted by the Bible, then as carrying its own legitimacy, and finally as so determining that, if reading the Bible continues as a cultural practice, it does so only within terms imposed by the newly dominant text.

This narrative of modernity as a series of relocated theories and practices of reading scripture begins with the concluding comments of the previous chapter concerning centrifugal reading, that aspect of reading the Bible that moves outward not only into the whole of the biblical text but into wider contexts as well. For Calvin, centrifugal reading arises from or follows on centripetal reading, for one does not remain in the space where the saving knowledge of God is imparted; one moves out from there to new understandings of biblical texts and to a reconstitution of the larger world. It is this outward movement that I now explore.

Three factors were crucial to this movement and emphasis. The first was the trope of the Book of Nature. This classical, medieval, and Renaissance notion was already there to be used, and Reformed leaders were not slow to pick it up. Already in the Belgic Confession (1561) this trope is redeployed in spreading the practice of reading Scripture outward to reading nature: "We know him . . . first by the creation, preservation, and government of the universe; which is before our eyes as a most elegant book, wherein all creatures, great and small, are as so many characters leading us to contemplate *the invisible things of God*, namely, *his eternal power and Godhead*."[1] The belief that nature not only could be read as a book but also should be read as a second scripture was anticipated by Calvin, readily available in the culture, and perfectly suited to the centrifugal movement of Reformed readers out into the larger world.

The second factor was Calvin's theory of accommodation, which he shared with Erasmus. This theory had two parts. First, it described the divine use of language. The language of the Bible, usually plain or direct and sometimes crude, accommodates God to humans and, in Calvin's metaphor, already mentioned, compares biblical language to that which an adult uses to speak to a child. But the theory of accommodation also implied that the writers of biblical texts accommodated themselves to understandings characteristic of the cultures in which they were writing. This theory of accommodation revealed the need and opportunity to reassess God's relation to the world in light of more recent learning.

The third factor in this exchange was the role in Calvin's work of the Old Testament generally and of the wisdom literature in particular. Calvin's strongly positive attitude toward the Old Testament allowed him to affirm the authority of wisdom literature. When centrifugal reading moved from the biblical texts out into interpretations of daily life and the surrounding world, it exited the biblical texts primarily by the doorway of wisdom literature. The wisdom literature provided an exit because biblical wisdom urged the reader to move from the text outward and to observe nature and society; it directed attention to and affirmed the authority of daily life and the natural context of human experience.

More important, substantial continuities were established between the principal interests of biblical wisdom and the new texts read as scripture. In a word, biblical wisdom directed attention to and warranted the three kinds of texts—nature, history, and literature—that should be read as scripture. But before detailing this point, I offer some general observations about wisdom literature that also are relevant to an appreciation of its importance for the modern period.

First, while wisdom literature contains materials from many sources, including popular culture, it is royal in its principal venue, and in the modern period this political/social quality granted legitimacy. Furthermore, there are close correlations between wisdom literature and the social/political spirit of the Renaissance and modern West because wisdom literature, associated biblically and in the Christian West specifically with Solomon, strongly supported the adventurous and expansionist political and cultural climate of emerging modernity.

Another general characteristic of the wisdom literature is that it identifies religious authority not so much with particular sacred objects, places, and times as with the complexities, resources, and exigencies of the quotidian world. In a very loose way it could be said, as Walter Brueggemann puts it, that the wisdom literature creates a culture of humanism and renaissance in Israel's history.[2] This in no way should be translated as a secularism; "fear of the Lord" plays a recurring role in this literature. But the movement of the wisdom is outward, and it extends well beyond—indeed it seems largely to disregard—the particular forms of religious authority that marked Israel's life. This sense of moving out beyond the circumference of religious structures to make discoveries in the surrounding world and to improvise appropriate responses to complex situations warranted, sponsored, or clarified modern culture's moves in several senses beyond the jurisdiction of religious institutions and into areas of new interest.

A third, general characteristic of the wisdom literature worth noting is that it carries a high regard for experience. The texts of wisdom, especially the Proverbs, defer to experience. Indeed, to be wise is not so much an ability to apply texts to cases as to read social situations and natural phenomena as texts, to study them. The teacher in Ecclesiastes is taught by experience what is important and what is not, and the student of wisdom in Proverbs is exhorted to go out and observe. Joseph, an exemplar of wisdom, moves into a new culture and has to make decisions on matters he never before encountered. Experience is normative, however, not in itself but because those who are wise are able to discern the work of God and divine directives in nature and history.

A final characteristic of wisdom is that it stresses the individual. While the individual in ancient cultures can never be taken as a counterpart to what in our culture the individual has become, it is striking that the exemplars of wisdom in the literature are people pretty much on their own: Joseph, Daniel, Job, Qoheleth, and the royal figures who are cited as sponsors, if not embodiments, of wisdom. This stress on the individual combines with the emphasis on experience, the lack of restraint imposed by religious institutions and authorities, and the expansionist attitudes to make wisdom texts enormously enabling for a culture that has characteristics analogous to all of these.

These general analogies between wisdom literature and the emerging culture may serve as a backdrop to the three principal preoccupations and loci of authority in wisdom. The first is the natural context of human life. The student in Proverbs is instructed to observe natural creatures. Job is to consider the cosmos and animal life in order to come to some sense of divine power. Nature in wisdom is a theological text, and reading it is a moral and spiritual discipline.

Second, wisdom directs the reader's attention to society and history. This can be seen, of course, in the royal histories, but it also pervades the literature. The student of wisdom in Proverbs is taught all along that society is complicated and that one should act in it with caution and restraint. Fools underestimate its complexity and act impulsively. Joseph in Egypt operates with efficient care in and through the complexities of Egyptian society and politics.

Finally, wisdom literature directs the reader's attention, especially in Proverbs, to wisdom itself as a transcendent ideal toward which humans should strive. Wisdom is posited as a possible future for humans and as a steady guide amidst perplexities. Wisdom is never fully and finally attained, but it is also not wholly beyond human reach.

The three principal "scriptures" of modernity—first nature, then history, and finally literature—are warranted in turn by each of these biblical wisdom emphases. The specific appeals to biblical wisdom texts, along with the general analogies that can be drawn between wisdom literature and an emerging modern culture, indicate that wisdom not only, by virtue of its outward thrust and direction, formed an exit from biblical texts to other texts but also indicated what in that larger world should be taken most seriously and how it should be read.

The three texts read as scripture appear in a serial order because reading nature as scripture was already in place as a cultural possibility in the sixteenth century by virtue of the trope of the Second Book. Human history appeared as scripture more slowly because it was not so clearly a text and not so clearly, as was nature, a text "written" by God. Literature was the last to appear as scripture because here clearly were texts written not by God but by human beings.

A second progression should also be traced. In each case, reading an extrabiblical text as scripture begins as biblically warranted. It then becomes a competing practice requiring negotiations of differences from and conflicts with reading the Bible. Finally, it usurps dominance, overshadowing and setting the terms for reading the Bible.

I

Readers of Francis Bacon will recall that Solomon, the biblical exemplar and patron of wisdom, figures prominently in his work. For those not so well acquainted, let me quote at some length from *The Advancement of Learning*: "So likewise in the person of Solomon [*sic*] the king, we see the gift or endorsement of wisdom and learning, both in Solomon's petition and in God's assent thereunto, preferred before all other terrane and temporal felicity. By virtue of which grant or donative of God Solomon became enabled not only to write those excellent parables or aphorisms concerning divine and moral philosophy; but also to compile a natural history of all verdure, from the cedar upon the mountain to the moss upon the wall (which is but a rudiment between putrefaction and an herb) [here Bacon is referring to and elaborating on 1 Kings 4:29–34], and also of all things that breathe or move. Nay, the same Salomon the king, although he excelled in the glory of treasure and magnificent buildings, of shipping and navigation, of service and attendance, of fame and renown, and the like, yet he maketh no claim to any of these glories, but only to the glory of inquisition of truth."³ Central to the culture and civilization projected by Bacon in the *New Atlantis* as ideal and that became the pattern for the Royal Society was "Salomon's House," which was the crown of all the excellent things created by its king. "Salomon's House" is dedicated to "the Works and Creatures of God," that is, to the study of nature. Among its treasures are texts written by Solomon that Christian lands of the West lack, especially Solomon's "Natural History which he wrote, of all plants, from the *cedar of Libanus* to the *moss that groweth out of the wall*, and of all *things that have life and motion*."⁴

Bacon was not limited to Solomon and to Proverbs in his use of the wisdom literature as warrant for his centrifugal move from the Bible outward to nature. As he says, "So likewise in that excellent book of Job, if it be revolved with diligence, it will be found pregnant and swelling with natural philosophy; as for example, cosmography, and the roundness of the world, *Qui extendit aquilonem super vacuum, et appendit terram super nihilum.*"[5] Bacon quotes extensively from Job, and Job is a strong theological warrant for Bacon's own interests because God directs Job to natural beings and events as loci of divine power and wisdom. Bacon also refers to wisdom psalms.

Bacon doubles his warrants for reading nature as scripture by including, along with the directives of biblical wisdom, the hoary trope of two books. Rather than refer to the tradition for this warrant, Calvin-like he refers to a biblical text: "For our Savior saith, 'You err, not knowing the scriptures, nor the power of God'; laying before us two books or volumes to study, if we will be secured from error; first the Scriptures, revealing the will of God, and then the creatures expressing his power."[6] This warrant appears in other crucial places, such as the *The New Organon*: "For he did not err who said, 'Ye err in that ye know not the Scriptures and the power of God,' thus coupling and blending in an indissoluble bond information concerning his will and meditation concerning his power [the Second Book]."[7] In his *Valerius Terminus* he asserts that when we read nature, we "lay . . . before us two books or volumes . . . if we will be secured from error; first the Scriptures revealing the word of God, and then the creatures expressing his power; for that latter book will certify us that nothing which the first teacheth shall be thought impossible."[8] It is clear from his formation of the relation between the Bible and the Book of Nature that Bacon sees the latter as supplementary to and warranted by the former.

The question that needs now to be asked is how this book of nature is to be read. The answer is that reading the book of nature in Bacon looks very much like reading as presupposed by Calvin's doctrine of Scripture. The difference lies not in the manner of reading but in what reading yields. For Bacon, centripetal reading of the Book of Nature leads not to saving knowledge but to knowledge of the simple constants by which the world was created and is maintained.

In addition, centripetal reading for Bacon, as for Calvin, undercuts the authority of institutions and previous interpretations. One does not read nature in a way directed by ecclesiastical and philosophical authorities but divests oneself of them while reading. Reading subverts the primacy both of the church and classical natural philosophy. Reading nature even subverts the authority of human language: "Here therefore is the first distemper of learning, when men study words and not matter. . . . for words are but the images of matter; and except they have life of reason and invention, to fall in love with them is all one as to fall in love with a picture." For Bacon, reading nature requires divestment of the preconceptions and inherited understandings conveyed by culture and language, for the sake of unprecedented or fresh knowledge; "if a man will begin with certainties, he shall end in doubts; but if he will be content to begin with doubts, he shall end in certainties." To encounter new and deeper truth, centripetal reading divests the inquirer of previous cultural conditioning. "For as the Psalms and other Scriptures do often invite us to consider and magnify the great and wonderful works of God, so if we should rest only in the contemplation of the exterior of them as they first offer themselves to our senses, we should do a like injury unto the majesty of God, as if we should judge or construe of the store of some excellent jeweller, by that only which is set out toward the street in his shop."[9] Indeed, a correspondence is set up between the reader's divestment of preconceptions and the move beyond the appearances of nature to the laws by which it was created and is ordered.

Bacon's centripetal reading of nature does not impart, as does Calvin's reading of the Bible, living knowledge of God but a knowledge of God that is indirect and impersonal. It is a knowledge of God that, in effect, God has left behind as traces from the creation of the world. Here is a fascinating gloss on Prov. 25:2: "[F]or so he [Solomon] saith expressly, 'The glory of God is to conceal a thing, but the glory of the king is to find it out'; as if, according to the innocent play of children, the Divine Majesty took delight to hide his works, to the end to have them found out; and as if kings could not obtain a greater honour than to be God's playfellows in that game; considering the great commandment of wits and means, whereby nothing need to be hidden from them."[10] This gloss is part of Bacon's defense of learning not as impious but as a response to God's implanted traces, a treasure hunt that leads to knowledge of God not otherwise available. The laws of nature are divine footsteps: "For God forbid that we should give out a dream of our own imagination for a pattern of the world; rather may he graciously grant to us to write an apocalypse or true vision *of the footsteps of the Creator imprinted on his creatures.*"[11] Centripetal reading of the book of nature, similar to Calvin's understanding of the centripetal reading of Scripture, involves an act of divestment by which a person is asked "to sweep away all theories and common notions, and to apply the understanding, thus made fair and even, to a fresh examination of particulars." As long as the reader lacks willingness to be so divested, human knowledge will continue to be "a mere medley and ill-digested mass, made up of much credulity and much accident, and also of the childish notions which we at first imbibed."[12] The end and reward of divestment is knowledge of those laws by which the world was made that lie as permanent traces left behind by God from the Creation. However, knowledge of God received in and by the centripetal reading of nature is fragmentary and acquired slowly by accumulation. The method "shall analyze experience and take it to pieces, and by a due process of exclusion and rejection lead to an inevitable conclusion."[13] Bacon compares such knowledge to a pyramid. The base is formed by natural history of the sort Solomon offers, the fruit of observation; the next stage is "physic," and the final "metaphysic." The point of the pyramid is the law of the works of God, "the summary law of nature." Bacon is not certain that humans can attain it, because the acts of reading are many and diverse and the process of induction from so many, differing readings is complicated and tentative.[14]

The centrifugal direction of reading nature sponsors an outward application of knowledge gained from centripetal reading to the human world. This application is trustworthy because the reader of nature has been internally affected by what has been read: "As touching the manners of learned men . . . it is not without truth which is said that *Abeunt studia in mores,* studies have an influence and operation upon the manners of those that are conversant in them."[15] Reading nature has beneficial moral consequences immediately for the reader and derivatively for society. Bacon relates centripetal to centrifugal reading by the metaphor of two conjoined planets, Saturn, the planet of contemplation, and Jupiter, the planet of action. The knowledge that is drawn from nature can be used for the "relief of man's estate."[16] He looks for fruitful consequences from the knowledge of God gained from reading nature, "a line and race of inventions that may in some degree subdue and overcome the necessities and miseries of humanity."[17] Centrifugal reading moves outward for Bacon no less extensively than it does in Calvin's reading of Scripture to a transformation of life, of society, and to some degree of the natural world.

Before leaving Bacon, two minor items in his work need to be mentioned because they have large consequences for what follows. The first deals with the question of the relative primacy of the two books and the reading of them. Bacon makes a subtle but important reapplication of Calvin's discussion of the relation of the knowledge of God found in observation of nature and history to the knowledge of God available only in reading the Bible. For Calvin, one who receives saving knowledge of God in reading the Bible would come as an altered person to the reading of nature and would read it in a truer way. But Bacon suggests that the reading of nature grants a person knowledge of God that prepares the person for reading the Bible. Reading nature even plays a requisite role by "not only opening our understanding to conceive the true sense of the scriptures, by the general notions of reason and rules of speech; but chiefly opening our belief, in drawing us into a due meditation on the omnipotency of God, which is chiefly signed and engraven upon his works."[18] This subtle point carries the potential of allowing the reading of nature to set terms for reading the Bible and the potential for making the Second Book not supplementary to the Bible but necessary to reading it aright. This point anticipates a shift in authority available already in the sixteenth century rather than much later.[19]

The second point that deserves mentioning is that Bacon anticipates the possibility of reading history along with nature as scripture. History can constitute such a text because reading nature produces advances in learning, discoveries, and inventions. When learning is limited by and to what already is known, when learning is largely or wholly learning what others wrote, then knowledge does not advance. As he says, "For as water will not ascend higher than the level of the first springhead from whence it descendeth, so knowledge derived from Aristotle, and exempted from liberty of examination, will not rise again higher than the knowledge of Aristotle."[20] Bacon implies that the study of nature generates learning as advance into the future.[21] The locus of interest shifts, therefore, from deference toward the past to outward and forward advancements of learning. This movement, supported and validated by reading the text of nature, stands in close relation to social and political advancement, assumed within it as an application of the fruits of natural knowledge.

John Locke plays a transitional role in this brief narrative of reading nature as though it were scripture. Raised a Puritan and espousing a strong belief in the indispensability and reliability of reading the Bible, Locke is also a pivotal figure for the rise of deism and the clear supremacy of reading nature as scripture. Although he holds reading the Bible and reading nature together, he does so in a way that threatens biblical primacy.

Locke's attack on innate ideas and his insistence that all knowledge comes to a person from without imply a theory of reading. By reading nature and the Bible one receives knowledge that is certain. But a shift in primacy occurs because for Locke knowledge received from reading nature can be trusted absolutely. Reading nature, or experience, as I pointed out earlier, is warranted by wisdom literature, but it carries for Locke its own certainty. The knowledge received from reading nature looks very much like the saving knowledge of God that for Calvin is directly imparted to the body of the reader in the centripetal reading of the Bible. Here is a typical passage from Locke, one employing the metaphor of inscription: "Let us then suppose the mind to be, as they say, white paper, void of all characters, without any ideas: How comes it to be furnished? Whence comes it by that vast store which the busy and boundless fancy of man has painted on it with an almost endless variety? Whence has it all the *materials* of reason and knowledge? To this I answer, in one word, from EXPERIENCE. In that all our knowledge is founded; and from it ultimately derives itself."[22] As with the *lectio divina*, the Book of Nature inscribes itself in the body of the reader. A text is created by imprints on the blank pages of the mind. These imprints are simple ideas. The resulting, imprinted text is wholly reliable, and all can be aligned with and tested by it.

Knowledge gained from reading the Bible, consequently, complements, rather than determines, the knowledge gained from nature and experience. "For faith can never convince us of anything that contradicts our knowledge. Because, though faith be founded on the testimony of God (who cannot lie) revealing any proposition to us: yet we cannot have an assurance of the truth of its being a divine revelation greater than our own knowledge." Reading the Bible, rather than validate the reading of nature, supplies certainty in areas that reading nature leaves as only probable: "[R]*evelation, where God has been pleased to give it, must carry it against the probable conjectures of reason.*" As Locke says later, "*Reason must be our last judge and guide in everything.*"[23] The category of things that can be known from revelation is established as supplemental by the knowledge received from a reading of nature.

In addition, Locke's reader will attribute primacy to the knowledge received from reading nature, because Locke is clear how such knowledge is received, while he is not clear how knowledge of spiritual things is received. The latter comes from the Bible, and Locke's "Reasonableness of Christianity" is a theology of atonement based on a reading primarily of the Gospels. But an acceptance of the saving knowledge that the Bible offers is dependent upon a prior belief in God, and it is not clear how that belief comes to a person or is warranted. It is my guess that Locke, like Calvin, simply assumes it as part of the culture and as necessary to it, that is, to human understanding and social interactions. In a word, he cannot conceive of operating without such a belief, so that it need not be accounted for. The Bible, for Locke, provides, as with Calvin, knowledge that God forgives, but in Locke this knowledge conforms to or is continuous with knowledge already in place from reading nature.

Locke labors to warrant what for us needs none, while he takes for granted what for us, who live in a culture that for more than a century now has provided those who want them ways of no longer believing in God, needs warranting. Locke introduces certainty in knowledge in order to give stability to religious life, which in his own time was rocked by dissension and excessive claims and demands on belief. Although he affirmed two sources of certainty—"But in such cases too we have reason and Scripture; unerring rules to know whether it be from God or no"[24]—the former stabilizes and verifies the latter.

Otherwise, Locke's theory of reading the Bible looks like Calvin's. The Bible should be read directly and not mediated by authority; reading the Bible should yield "plain direct meaning" rather than fanciful and willful interpretation or "systems of divinity, according to the notions that each one has been bred up in."[25] And, like Calvin, Locke emphasizes a minimalist or centripetal reading of the Bible, although in Locke this minimal reading has as its yield the *proposition* that Jesus is the Messiah. Furthermore, while for Calvin saving knowledge of God's grace is imparted to the reader by the Holy Spirit, for Locke it is more a conclusion drawn from the work and words of Jesus. Locke makes much of the fact that the disciples did not come to believe that Jesus was the Messiah because he said so but because they inferred it from what he said and did: "It was not fit to open himself too plainly or forwardly to the heady jews, that he himself was the Messiah: that was to be left to the observation of those, who would attend to the purity of his life, the testimony of his miracles, and the conformity of all with the predictions concerning him."[26] However, as in Calvin, centripetal reading is followed by working out in the world the life of obedience that follows from belief in Jesus as Messiah.

A subtle but pivotal shift can also be seen in Locke's treatment of the Pauline epistles, to which he gave special and extended attention. Locke advocates in the reading of the Pauline epistles ways of coming to understand not so much God, the Kingdom of Christ, or the objects of faith as Paul's beliefs and thoughts.[27]

Locke, consequently, becomes the site of a transition or exchange. Although he appeals to the Bible as the source of everything that one "wishes to know concerning the nature of God and the reason for man's moral obligation to follow the law of nature," although "the vital centre of Locke's moral thought [is] the Holy Scriptures," and although "all the roads of Lockean philosophy [do] lead to the hallowed ground of Christianity,"[28] Locke placed reading the Bible within the context of his theories of knowledge, which have certainty as their principal preoccupation.[29] The attention he gives to reading the text of nature and experience and the certainty to which that reading leads set the conditions for reading the Bible as scripture. Locke, consequently, allows for such directions as Toland's *Christianity Not Mysterious* (1696) takes and that so many in the next century followed.

By the end of the next century this exchange is complete, and no clearer statement of it could be made than is made by Tom Paine's *Age of Reason*. It is important to note how goals and criteria used in Calvin's doctrine of Scripture appear in Paine's argument that one should read not the Bible but nature if one is to read the word of God. Clarity is one of them; as Calvin characterized the Bible as making clear what otherwise is blurry, Paine argues that nature makes clear what the Bible obscures. In addition, Calvin wanted to take reading the Bible out of the confines of clerical privilege and to make it available to every Christian. Paine believes that reading the Bible is a clerical privilege because it needs to be explained by experts to ordinary people, but nature is open for everyone to read and to understand. Much of the power of Paine's argument for reading nature as scripture derives from his employment of principles basic to the status of Bible reading in the lives of Christians. In addition, of course, Paine was talking to fellow Americans for whom the appeal of anticlericalism, even outside Quaker circles, had continuing potential, for whom democratic values were life-and-death issues, and for whom nature was, as well as a religious datum, also a principal characteristic and point of distinction of the new nation.

Readers of the Book of Nature discern God in the text because nature was written not by human but by divine hand: "Search not the book called the Scripture, which any human hand might make, but the Scripture called Creation," he says.[30] And the text of nature can be read without clerical mediation and interpretation. It is available and perspicuous to all.[31] Paine finds the conclusion to be irresistible: "THE WORD OF GOD IS THE CREATION WE BEHOLD."[32]

The act of reading nature for Paine is first of all centripetal. Not only does this mean coming to the text free from the confinements of tradition, it also means reading nature not so much in terms of its surfaces and diversity but, as in Bacon, in terms of its underlying principles. These principles bring the reader close to knowledge of God, for the principles of science are approximations of the laws by which the world was created: "Every science has for its basis a system of principles as fixed and unalterable as those by which the universe is regulated and governed. Man cannot make principles, he can only discover them." Paine uses traditional examples from mathematics and geometry to illustrate his point: "Man had no more to do in the formation of these properties or principles, than he had to do in making the laws by which the heavenly bodies move; and therefore the one must have the same Divine origin as the other." These principles, available to the centripetal reader, "are the foundation of all the science that exists in the world, and must be the foundation of theology."[33]

Paine's argument is extreme not because he claims that nature can and should be read as scripture—this is part of the tradition and basic to Bacon—but because he is so vigorous and unrelenting in displanting Bible reading with reading nature. His attack on the Bible is many-pronged, but a major argument draws on the tradition, introduced by Bacon and certified by Locke, in which human language is not only secondary but also suspect for communicating knowledge. Since human language is chronologically and logically secondary, reading nature directly subverts the false primacy not only of ecclesiastical and philosophical learning but also of human language. "Learning," Paine says, "does not consist, as the schools now make it consist, in the knowledge of languages, but in the knowledge of things to which language gives names." Language, moreover, is inseparable from human interests and contingencies: "The continually progressive change to which the meaning of words is subject, the want of a universal language which renders translation necessary, the errors to which translations are again subject, the mistakes of copyists and printers, together with the possibility of willful alteration, are of themselves evidences that human language, whether in speech or in print, cannot be the vehicle of the word of God."[34] For Paine, the Word of God and human language have a contrary relation to one another, and human language needs constantly to be divested and reconstituted by reading nature. This denigration of language not only serves to divorce reading nature from biblical warrants but also dissolves the metaphors of book and reading that had sustained the cultural investment in the study of nature. The loss of these metaphors opens the way for a science dissociated not only from theories of textuality and reading but also from culture altogether.

The weight Paine places on discrediting human language as a locus of divine revelation can be seen, also, in the argument he mounts against miracles. Rather than argue against them because they are exceptions to the laws of nature, Paine argues that their credibility rests on their reporters and that the credibility of biblical writers can be questioned because of the morally objectionable practices that they condoned: "But when I see throughout the greater part of this book scarcely anything but a history of grossest vices and a collection of the most paltry and contemptible tales, I cannot dishonor my Creator by calling it by his name." Indeed, the Bible has developed a religion and a culture among its readers that is objectionable: "Of all the systems of religion that ever were invented, there is none more derogatory to the Almighty, more unedifying to man, more repugnant to reason, and more contradictory in itself, than this thing called Christianity. Too absurd for belief, too impossible to convince, and too inconsistent for practice, it renders the heart torpid, or produces only atheists and fanatics."[35] Bound by human language and culture to a secondary or derivative position, marked by human contingencies, and implicated in the evils of a history produced by it, the Bible is a text unworthy, especially when compared to nature, to be read as scripture. The choice for Paine is obvious. On the one side is a humanly conditioned, textually corrupted, morally and intellectually offensive text read for centuries as a way to promote ignorance and dependence and to warrant cruelty and exploitation, and on the other side is a book written by God, available for all to read, reliable, edifying, and productive of morality.

It is fascinating, given his attack on reading the Bible, that Paine uses excerpts from biblical texts to strengthen his position. The excerpts are taken, of course, from wisdom literature. He uses parts of Job to warrant the theological importance of the Creation and extends this point to include Psalm 19. He quotes from Proverbs and uses the wisdom material included by Matthew in the Sermon on the Mount. He takes these texts to be exceptions to his general characterization of the Bible, and he even suggests that some of these texts are so different from the rest as perhaps to have been written by gentiles and to have been incorporated later into the Bible.

Paine's use of wisdom literature, the importance for him of belief in God as creator, and his conception of the moral life as a necessary and fit response to the Creation by those who read nature as scripture indicate how appropriate it is to identify him as a sapiential theologian. Paine's moves carry the orientation of biblical wisdom, namely, to identify the locus of divine power and wisdom not in a particular event, place, or artifact but in the Creation. Paine, however, cuts away the biblical warrants for his move to nature by defending it not only as independent from biblical texts but also as largely in opposition to them. Paine points to the nineteenth century and the eventual demise not only of biblical support for reading nature as scripture but also of reading nature as a text. This ends in projection, primarily in terms of ownership and use, of human interests onto "nature" and in the domination and appropriation of nature. Intellectually it means the control of science by the experimental method, and culturally it means the eventual loss of continuity between human language and the natural context of human life. In our own century these consequences are virtually "naturalized."

II

How it came about that history was taken as a "Second Book" that could be read as scripture alongside the Bible and how it gained cultural dominance over reading the Bible is not easily recounted, because it is not so clearly documented. However, the direction of sixteenth-century culture was unquestionably outward, a direction to which Calvinism contributed by means of centrifugal reading. This outward, forward direction was accelerated by Bacon, who projected a development of consequences for the application of human knowledge to nature. Centrifugal reading, the growth of science, and the lure of discovery made temporal movement characteristic of the culture.

The question, however, is how the interests of modern culture were turned not only toward the future and recent advancements of learning but also toward the distant past. How does a preoccupation with history become characteristic of modern culture?

One contributing factor, of course, which arose from the new learning, has to do with an increased respect for ancient texts shorn of accumulated and often authoritative interpretations. The strong desire to get back to more original situations, to free the past from the mediation of intervening interests, was intensified by the parallel quest for the laws behind the surfaces of nature. J.G.A. Pocock points to an additional factor relating the study of history to the search for constants. He suggests that the faculties of law in the French universities of the early sixteenth century generally had a high regard for the classical world but had to distinguish within it structures that no longer pertained to their own time from those, especially Roman law, that actually or potentially did. He suggests that this careful attention to the distant past and the need to distinguish the constant from the contingent in history initiated historiography as we know it.[36]

The further question is how it came about that the histories of nonbiblical people, of people separate from histories recounted by and related to the Bible, came to be read as scripture. Hans Frei offers help by indicating in the work of Johannes Cocceius (1603–69) a move away from occupation with biblical narratives and toward an emerging interest in general human history. Frei takes this shift of interest toward a temporal reality other than the biblical as initiating a separation of biblical from general history and an increasing domination of the former by the latter.[37]

The first major attempt to establish the history of nonbiblical people as a second scripture was made by Giambattista Vico, who derived inspiration for this move from Bacon.[38] Vico deliberately tries to do for history what Bacon did for the reading of nature. Like Bacon, he establishes the practice of reading another text as scripture alongside of and complementary to the Bible. Vico does not question the primacy or reliability of history recorded by the Bible for an understanding of the Hebrew people and early Christians.[39] What Vico does is to construct a second text, the history of the gentile nations, which he posits as scripture because reading it reveals not the special grace of God shown in biblical and Christian history but a general grace, namely, Providence. This second scripture gives knowledge of God that otherwise would be unavailable, and Vico deliberately compares it to, even favors it over, the kind of knowledge of God that Bacon and those who follow him derive from their readings of nature.[40] Principally, the text of history grants knowledge of the laws and social structures that make it possible for people to live with one another in relative peace and order.[41] Finally, Vico, like Bacon, warrants this construction of a second scripture on the basis of wisdom, which Vico takes, like Bacon, as directing the reader's attention to the revelatory potential of the work of God in the natural order of things, an interest that produces in the reader of history as much as the reader of nature a desire for wisdom.[42]

Vico constructs his history of the gentile nations against the grain by arguing that, contrary to the notions that these nations have of their pasts, they were not originally innocent but were bestial and driven by self-interests.[43] This means that the development of law and social order cannot be accounted for on the basis of human nature. Peace and order in gentile history can only be accounted for by the work of Providence. The history of the gentile nations, then, becomes a second scripture because it reveals an event that humans on their own could not have caused, namely, the development of human societies. Vico believes that this reading of gentile history is not forced by the reader; the providential work of God is there to be read, although it must be read against the grain of people's own accounts of their histories.

While the focus on Providence, due to its emphasis on divine power and control, carries a potential problem for Vico as a Catholic, he does not address the relation of Providence to human will directly but assumes a mediating position between divine determination and human will and chance.[44] He allows the relation of these forces to be inferred from rather than imposed on the text.[45] Finally, the chief characteristic of Providence, like the traces of the Creator discerned by readers of nature, is to provide order. Providence is "a divine legal mind," and Vico's history is "a rational civil theology of divine providence."[46] Consequently, history becomes a second scripture that grants the reader knowledge of the works of God.

The patterns that Vico contends diverse nations have in common substantiate his claim that what one reads in the histories of the gentile nations is the work of God. Since God is one, the striking differences between peoples need to be countered by at least some shared order, and Vico thinks he knows what that is. The recurring and shared patterns in the development of various societies, which Vico is famous for noting, are what diverse peoples and histories can be seen to share, given that a single Providence is operative within them.[47]

The patterns and laws that Vico points out as common to the development and constitutions of diverse societies are so easily extractable because he so deliberately and repeatedly refers to and contends for them. Indeed, his *New Science* has far more to do with shared patterns and laws than with the diverse histories of gentile nations. This is due to the argument that Vico is making for reading the history of gentile nations as a complementary scripture, one in which the work of God can be recognized and acknowledged. By reading the texts of the gentile nations as documents in which Providence can be seen as working, Vico offers history as a second scripture to be read with a twofold result: first, the texts of the special history of Hebrews and Christians from Adam down can be joined to the complementary scripture, and second, Christians can read this complementary scripture in order to gain a wider knowledge of God that will enhance piety.[48]

Like Locke, who no less than Vico thought of what he was doing as dependent upon reading the Bible as scripture, Vico presents theories that can be detached from their biblical warrant. This is because Vico does not articulate the relation between his theory of reading history as a text within which the laws of Providence can be read and reading the Bible.[49] It is simply incorporated in his work along with Bacon. Both Locke and Vico, consequently, played transitional roles because they were eager to secure what those who followed them readily accepted and used, while they did not secure but simply assumed warrants that those who followed them began to doubt and discount.

Hegel uses Vico in his theory of reading history as scripture. Like Vico, he relates history to Providence and Providence to wisdom.[50] Hegel shares Vico's admiration for Bacon and joins Vico in elevating the text of history over the text of nature as an account of divine wisdom: "It was for awhile the fashion to profess admiration for the wisdom of God, as displayed in animals, plants, and isolated occurrences. But, if it be allowed that Providence manifests itself in such objects and forms of existence, why not also in Universal History?" Hegel's major departure from Vico is to posit one history inclusive of both biblical history and the histories of the gentile nations. That single history, moreover, is one to which biblical history in its particularity must defer and in relation to which it must be interpreted. As a consequence, the providential and soteriological works of God are combined into one text. "Only *this* insight can reconcile Spirit with the History of the World—viz., that what has happened, and is happening every day, is not only not 'without God,' but is essentially His Work"—the concluding assertion of the *Philosophy of History*.[51]

Reading history is not only a way of coming to knowledge of God, it is also a way of cooperating with the process of God's self-revelation, because reading history is how the effects of Providence are actualized. Reading history is part of history because events and the reading of events are not separable. Hegel takes it as significant that the word for history means both the events and the way events are read or related to patterns by people who observe them. The two, events and historical accounts, arise together.[52] Since the unfolding of history and the account of that unfolding have everything to do with one another, Hegel also does not think there is an accidental relation between his attempt to give a universal account of history and the stage of history's unfolding that he finds himself in, a stage that began, as he points out in the last part of the *Philosophy of History*, with the German Reformation. This puts a particularly forceful emphasis on reading for Hegel, which Mark C. Taylor describes in a way that recalls the practice of *lectio divina*: "The elevation of the material to the spiritual and the return of objectivity to subjectivity take place through a process of incorporation or 'inwardization' (*Erinnerung*) akin to eating and reading. To read the living word truly is to be nourished by the spirit that translates from death to life. . . . For life to be complete, consumption must be total. If spiritual reading is to erase every trace of the written word, there must be nothing left over—no crumbs or fragments, surely no philosophical crumbs or fragments."[53] Reading is participation, an action that produces change.

The principal effect of universal history is the actualization of freedom. Hegel does not define this freedom individually, however; like Vico, he is impressed by the remarkable importance of social and political order among people who are otherwise driven by individual impulses. The relation of individual freedom to corporate order should be balanced, and the one should find realization in the other.[54] When that occurs, "Society and the State are the very conditions in which Freedom is realized."[55] Arresting instances of this balance occur when such individuals as political leaders, artists, or philosophers intuit the direction of Providence and lead people out of structures that have begun to confine freedom by becoming mere custom.

The State, inclusive of culture and of attachments persons feel toward homeland and history, is the counterpart of the individual, and States are the individuals that go into the development of universal history.[56] But the State is not fixed; it itself, along with everything else, is a part of the great unfolding. This unfolding is not only complex, it is also dialectical. That is, it is a process by which contraries emerge and are transcended. This process means that the course of universal history is upward as well as outward, increasingly inclusive and higher. This process is not straightforward, a gradual emerging of the more perfect from the less. What is left behind is also rejected, although that which rejects depends on what is left behind and takes something of it along. This makes the process of history, while it is basically good and marked by advance, painful. Although history is the work of God and although humans participate in that work, humans are not, when they participate, happy. History is marked by struggle, alienation, and conflict.

Not all participate in the work of God. Catholics, by clinging to outmoded and confining structures and by perpetuating forms of authority and dependence, resist the work of God, and Africans are not yet included in history. While history is universal, its fullest manifestation, the actualization of freedom, occurs in northern Europe and, one would suppose, in Hegel's philosophy. The power of history to comprehend particular forms also justifies Hegel's replacement of reading the Bible with reading history as scripture. While he applauds the Reformers for giving the Bible into the hands of individual Christians and for giving Christians a way to subvert the authority of the church, the Bible nevertheless has its limitations, which now have been transcended.[57] Reading history, for Hegel, displaces reading the

Bible as scripture, and it sets the terms for what remains of value in reading the Bible.

Julius Wellhausen provides a clear and influential example of the dominance of reading history as scripture over reading the Bible. Wellhausen reads history as a text that counters the Bible because he believes that the Bible often advocates institutions and their functionaries that, for Wellhausen, not only are derivative from the creative historical effects of individuals and the spontaneous response of people to natural occurrences, but also have a deadening effect on them. His *Prolegomena to the History of Ancient Israel* does not merely make a scholarly observation about the late formation of the priestly material and its lack of precedent in ancient Israel but also retells biblical history according to how Wellhausen believes history actually is made. Reading is a way of rescuing history from the control of institutions and priests. Early in his discussion Wellhausen refers in more than one way to the "Priestly code" as "our problem."[58]

When he contrasts priests with prophets, Wellhausen deploys his theory of the primacy not only in ancient Israel but in all history of creative individuals. Rather than rest, as do priests, on a status granted to them by someone or something else, the prophets stand on their own; indeed it can be said that "representative men are always single, resting on nothing outside themselves. We have thus on the one side the tradition of a class . . . and on the other the inspiration of awakened individuals, stirred up by occasions which are more than ordinary." Institutions preserve and perpetuate the work of individuals but in the process fix and deaden it; the prophets, on the other hand, "live in the storm of the world's history, which sweeps away human institutions." "It belongs," he concludes, "to the notion of prophecy, of true revelation, that Jehovah, overlooking all the media or ordinances and institutions, communicates Himself to the *individual*, the called one, in whom that mysterious and incredible rapport in which the deity stands with men clothes itself with energy."[59] Compared to that of prophets, the work of priests can be seen as "artificial," as marked by "pedantry," and as characterized by "senility."[60]

Not only does Wellhausen see the bulk of the Old Testament as under the petrifying hand of priests, he also sees priestly interests as central to the development of Judaism. There is, then, a sharp contrast constructed in the text not only between layers of biblical texts but also between postexilic Judaism and ancient Israel. Wellhausen wants no doubt left about this difference: "Judaism, which realized the Mosaic constitution and carried it out logically, left no free scope for the individual; but in ancient Israel the divine right did not attach to the institution but was in the Creator Spirit, in individuals. Not only did they speak like the prophets, they also acted like the judges and kings, from their own free impulse, not in accordance with an outward norm, and yet, or just because of this, in the Spirit of Jehovah."[61] He traces what he considers to be not a natural evolution of priestly influence in Israel but the concentration of religious authority as an act of political power and as coincident with the demise of Israel's spiritual integrity and confidence.[62]

Wellhausen argues that the centralization and urbanization of the cultus, rather than lift the religion of Israel above the paganism of its Canaanite context and the practices of other peoples to a more spiritual level, as Moshe Weinfeld recently has contended,[63] made Judaism more like "heathen" cultures than the religion of ancient Israel ever had been. In addition, the difference between Greek and Hebrew, a difference that Hegel, of course, had made much of, becomes a difference not only in principle but in detail.[64]

Finally, Wellhausen is eager to point out similarities between what Judaism did to the religion of ancient Israel and what Roman Catholicism did to the religion of the early church. He remarks sarcastically at one point, for example, that "Moses is the originator of the Mosaic constitution in about the same way as Peter is the founder of the Roman hierarchy," that is, not at all or else only by distortion.[65]

The irresistible conclusion of Wellhausen's argument is not only that the Bible is to be read with suspicion but that the Bible, like an institution, always is secondary to history as it is made by or epitomized in the lives of representative individuals. Institutions and texts live off these accomplishments and transpose the spirit of individuals into class and institutional authority. As with Paine's attack on the Bible, Wellhausen's position is an implicit attack on all texts as derivative and as unavoidably tainted by self-interest in distinction from history as it actually is. Individuals are crucial to history because in them the Creator Spirit speaks or comes to visibility. This same Spirit has the consequence of liberating the reader of history from the distortions imposed on it by institutions and their functionaries.

Hegel's affirmation that institutional objectification of the Spirit had to be overcome in a dialectical process of spiritual expansion gave new meaning to the conflicts discerned in the early church between the putative particularism and institutionalism of Jewish Christianity and the universality and forward direction of gentile Christian history. F. C. Baur sees this historical movement as taken up by Protestantism, where the overcoming of the particular and the institutional by the universal and the spiritual carries forward the victory of Pauline Christianity over that of Peter and James. Paul was, he says, "the originator and exponent of that which constitutes the essence of Christianity as distinguished from Judaism."[66]

Bruno Bauer is more explicit in drawing an antagonistic relation between Christianity and Judaism, seeing the latter as impeding the process of history and the ever-enlarging human consciousness that is its consequence. Indeed, Bauer went on from this opposition between Judaism and Christianity and between Catholicism and Protestantism to a general attack on religion in the name of history as expanding self-consciousness.[67] Adolf Harnack similarly saw Paul as a liberator of Christianity from Judaism, with Marcion completing Paul's work.[68] Harnack, like Hegel and Wellhausen, employed, in opposition to institutionalization, a "great-man" theory of history, and great men, along with whatever else they teach, bring the liberating message of historical advance by means of individual creativity. A well-known extension of this theory into biblical studies, of course, is the work of Albert Schweitzer, who found, within the unusable textual husks of ancient worldviews, heroes, such as Jesus, who made a difference in history— "We must go back," he concludes, "to the point where we can feel again the heroic in Jesus . . . only then can the heroic in our Christianity and in our 'Weltanschauung' be again revived."[69]

Displacing the emphasis in these theories on the role of "great men" in the dynamics of historical advance is a gradual sense of separation between history, with its political, social, and economic force, and personal potential and needs. Rather than a coincidence between the individual and history, an increasing alienation is posited, tying self-actualization to removal from history. One finds this fully articulated in the biblical studies of Rudolf Bultmann, for whom human freedom is not only discontinuous with history but even contrary to it.[70]

This displacement reveals the loss in our century of reading history as scripture. This loss has been accelerated by rapid urbanization, industrialization, imperialism, and warfare. The increasingly contrary relation that develops in late-nineteenth- and twentieth-century culture between history and the cultural need or desire for meaning and identity is crucial to the next phase of the narrative. History, no longer read as though it were scripture, like nature, becomes something to be claimed and appropriated. Neither nature nor history carries coherence or significance other than what people project onto them primarily by the use they make of them.

III

Reading literature as scripture makes a late appearance because, unlike nature and history, which could be read as texts written by God, literature is humanly produced. The crucial ingredients behind this chapter in the narrative were analogues between the writers of literature and the "great men" who made history and between human and divine creativity. In the second half of the eighteenth century literature began to be treated as a text that could be read as scripture.[71] However, such treatment was secured by the Romantics, and a major document is Coleridge's *Biographia Literaria,* whose principal source, in its turn, was Immanuel Kant.

Kant bases his critique of aesthetic judgment on the tradition of reading nature as scripture rather than reading works of art as scripture. He begins with nature, and he does not think that judgments about fine art are different from—indeed, they seem to require as their warrant and clarification—judgments about the beauty of nature. In addition, nature is noted particularly for making available moments of the sublime. Nature more than humanly created works of art offers such occasions. Kant's analysis of the complex state of mind occasioned by natural scenes of great power or size distinguishes stages, primarily a move from negative to positive states of mind. As he says, "[T]he feeling of the sublime is a pleasure that only rises indirectly, being brought about by the feeling of a momentary check to the vital forces followed at once by a discharge all the more powerful, and so it is an emotion that seems to be no sport, but dead earnest in the affairs of the imagination."[72] The state of mind produced in moments of the sublime is serious and complex.[73] Consequently, Kant relates the perception of the sublime to morality.

The crucial move for Kant is from analysis of the perception of the beautiful and the sublime in nature to analysis of their perception in things humanly made. It is not clear on what this move is based. It is not that Kant had a developed appreciation for fine art; many commentators point out his minimal interests in music and painting. Perhaps, although I do not know of anyone who has suggested this, he moves from nature to humanly made works by means of formal gardens, since they were so developed and prominent an art form in the eighteenth century. The move is also, of course, dependent on Kant's understanding of the perception of beauty in nature. The human capacity for aesthetic pleasure occasioned by nature seems to suggest the human capacity as well to create. Rationality and idea are crucial to both, and the capacity for aesthetic pleasure indicates the capacity, stimulated by the perception of beauty in nature, to create beautiful things.

Basic to aesthetic pleasure in works of art (Kant includes, as well, perception of beauty in crafts and ordinary artifacts) is form. Form here is Aristotelian; form is inherent. The pleasure of the beautiful is derived from the perception of its final form. This form, perceived in a work of art, cannot be accounted for by factors outside itself or exhaustively conceptualized. This is not because the perception of beauty is devoid of ideas; rather, the ideas are aesthetic. They stand in contrast to rational ideas in that they cannot be conceptually conveyed and cannot be separated from their occasions.[74] Aesthetic ideas have a quickening effect on the mind, are exemplary, and stimulate creativity. In this way, works of art are productive of one another.

The form of a work of fine art is granted to it by its creator in a way, it seems, analogous to the final form perceived in the creation of natural objects. Form cannot be accounted for by means of some rule or combination of factors; it is original and must be attributed to something extraordinary in the human mind or to human minds that are extraordinary. Rather than exercise the first option, which would have provided a transition from the perception of beauty to creating it, Kant exercises the second and attributes such works to genius. The creative person takes on a position, therefore, that is analogous to that of the Creator in relation to nature, and this move imputes powerful and significant possibilities to reading works of art as scripture.

Three aspects of Kant's critique are most important for warranting the reading of literature as though it were scripture, then: the autonomy and power of aesthetic ideas and their inseparable relation to what occasions them, the pleasure of perceiving final form as an end in itself, and the relation of creative genius to the transcendent.[75]

The *Biographia Literaria* is a literary manifesto of the sort ordinarily associated with the announcements of radical departures issued by artists a century later. Coleridge decisively distinguishes poetry as it now is, that is, poetry as it ought to be, from poetry as it once was, particularly in the former century. Formerly, poetry was subject to the artificial interests of society. Poetry was characterized not by poetic thoughts but by nonpoetic thoughts that were translated into the language of poetry. His accusations of artificiality and of nonpoetic, or prose, thoughts are particularly pointed.[76]

Coleridge acknowledges his indebtedness to Kant several times.[77] Using Kant on one side and Wordsworth, as exemplary of genius, on the other, he deploys his theory of reading poetry as scripture. The marks of genius are the ability to unite deep feeling with profound thought, ordinary incidents with the ideal, and accurate observation of details with modifications that heighten them.[78] Genius is even more to be valued given what Coleridge regards as the general level to which literature and its role in society had sunk. Indeed, a contrary relation is established between social history and the texts of poetic genius.

Of central importance for Coleridge in the genius of Wordsworth is the power available in reading his poetry for combining diverse or contrary matters. For this reason he enters long disquisitions on theories of association in various philosophers from Descartes down. The contraries that intrigue him most, due at least in part to his interest in Descartes, are the subjective, or internal, and the objective, or external. Also important are the contraries of active and passive associations, associations that a person creates and those that are given. Coleridge is particularly interested in the internal side of the first and the passive side of the second set of contraries. He is intrigued by the vast "text" that is created by the "collective experience" of a person, containing imperishably all that a person has sensed and thought. This "text" makes experience possible and contributes heavily to knowledge. Knowledge, indeed, arises from the interplay of occasions of experience and this antecedent text of memory.[79] Knowledge, then, is a matter of combining the objective and subjective or being and knowing.

The cause and manner of this combining cannot for Coleridge be specified, and attempts to do so trivialize it.[80] Indeed, he uses religious language to designate this mysterious, enabling power. Its nature and role are further complicated by the fact that it creates both identity between subject and object, or internal and external, and antithetical relations between them so that the subjective can become an object. By this means we become self-conscious. Since this faculty or factor is both crucial to our sense of self and is so mysterious, Coleridge concludes that reflection on self leads one to God and that "true metaphysics are nothing else but true divinity."[81]

All of this is crucial to the famous closing paragraphs of chapter 13, on the primary and secondary Imagination and their difference from Fancy. The associations effected by Fancy are governed by laws and by a repertoire of definites. An act of the secondary Imagination "dissolves, diffuses, dissipates, in order to re-create" and is vital, although it works with and on materials that are fixed and dead. The primary Imagination, however, because it not only is vital but also combines vitalized material, is truly creative and is "a repetition in the finite mind of the eternal act of creation in the infinite

I AM."[82] Because of this repetition, the act of creation is at the same time an act of full self-actualization, although the self that is actualized is not one's self but that mystery of combination that leads to or instantiates the divine. Poetry is singled out from the general discussion of the aesthetic in Kant because for Coleridge language carries most fully the relation of the subjective and objective to one another and because symbolic language has the capacity to combine contraries. Indeed, language is for Coleridge potentially "esemplastic," by which he means that it can bring together many things, especially the contraries of the one and the many.[83] Language has a special relation for Coleridge to the mind itself, and it is formed by the appropriation of fixed symbols and by acts of the Imagination "the greater part of which have no place in the consciousness of uneducated man."[84] And nothing stands alongside or above poetry as a counter to genius, as taste and judgment in Kant stand as correctives to creativity. Indeed, as truth is the only way to measure truth, so it is "the prerogative of poetic genius to distinguish" what is pure poetry from what is not. Could the rules for distinguishing pure poetry be objectified, they would turn poetry into a mechanical act.[85] The Imagination is its own legislator and governor.

Also distinguishing Coleridge from Kant—specifically, from the contrast Kant draws between Rational and Aesthetic ideas—is the contrast Coleridge draws between poetry, primarily its capacity for vital combinations and the access it grants to that in language which imparts the divine to human life, and technology. What we get in Wordsworth and Coleridge is a social critique that puts poetry into a dissonant relation with historical changes. Poetry's primacy is implicitly defended on the demise of history as a text to be read as scripture.

In this manifesto poetry, by granting access to genius, relates the reader to divinity. Literature has a salvific potential and ought to be read as though it were scripture. However, Coleridge does have a high view of the Bible. Like others I have considered, Coleridge deploys a theory that is supported by assumptions about the Bible as scripture that he would not want to threaten, and his literary theory and theories of language are supported by his high estimation of the Bible, its languages, the people who wrote it, and its religious and theological content. Indeed, it can be said that his *Confessions of an Inquiring Spirit,* which concentrates on reading the Bible, parallels the *Biographia,* which concentrates on writing poetry.[86] But like theories of Locke and Vico, his theory of poetry can easily be separated from its biblical parallels and warrants and can be deployed not only by itself but as a counter to the practice of reading the Bible as scripture. This, it seems to me, is what happens in the process by which literature, as with nature and history earlier, comes to be read instead of the Bible as scripture.

Matthew Arnold, also using the contrast between history and genius, proposes a role for reading poetry that, as Lionel Trilling observes, continues to shadow literary studies well into the twentieth century.[87] Indeed, its influence, along with Coleridge's, is felt to the present day. This is due not only to the range of his project; it is due also to his cultural analysis and criticism and to his conclusion that literature and literary criticism must assume the role in the formation of culture once played by religion and theology. Arnold charts a course for reading literature as though it were scripture, a course analogous to that of the deists for nature and Hegel for history.

The sense of urgency that Arnold creates arises from a crisis he claims that English culture faces. Increasingly marked by materialism and by a habit of mistaking means for ends, the culture is drifting toward a mediocrity that resists great poetry. The current culture empowers people with money and a sense of freedom without directing these powers toward significant ends. The result is that the culture becomes hostage to the vulgar, unstable, and contentious. Social fragmentation and class divisions along with individuals and groups who assert their particular interests create a situation that threatens culture as a whole. The result is a society at once both flattened and fragmented. This defines more than anything else what Arnold means by "anarchy." It is not a culture in which great poetry can emerge to do its work.[88]

The role of criticism must be to help create a culture fit for great poetry. The general marks of such a criticism are the following: it brings to attention by means of selection and concentration the best that is known and thought in the world; it focuses attention on the future, particularly on the perfection of human life; it fosters clear-sightedness, an ability to see things as they are, even to question beneficent causes for their want of spiritual direction; it manages the just proportion of its two principal qualities, namely, its biblical inheritance concerning work, direction, and morality, what Arnold calls Hebraism, and its classical-Renaissance inheritance concerning spontaneity and thought; and it combines social inclusiveness with authority and purpose.[89]

In order to accomplish these things, the critic must be disinterested, must keep aloof from particular and practical interests and follow "the law of [criticism's] own nature, which is to be a free play of the mind on all subjects which it touches."[90] Most of all, the critic must be a reader. Arnold stresses the practice of reading in his major text on religion, "Literature and Dogma: An Essay Towards a Better Apprehension of the Bible." The culture the critic sponsors is based on a reading that, while it includes the Bible, moderates the Bible's contribution by placing it in relation to other texts. Culture determines what is needed from religion in general and from the Bible in particular.[91] He says that "culture is *reading*; but reading with a purpose to guide it, and with system."[92] That purpose and goal are epitomized by the state. The state is the form of inclusiveness that will overcome fragmentation and particularism, and it has the authority or power to counteract the force of anarchy: "We want an authority, and we find nothing but jealous classes, checks, and a deadlock; culture suggests the idea of *the State*. We find no basis for a firm State-power in our ordinary selves; culture suggests one to us in our *best self*."[93]

That toward which all of this must be directed is not some already existing entity or already defined purpose. The goal is always in the future, always transcendent. The goal, in a word, is the full actualization of the human spirit, humanity as a "harmonious perfection." The goal is "not a having and a resting, but a growing and a becoming."[94] This means that the aim of culture coincides with religion.

It is very important to notice that in "Literature and Dogma" Arnold, when he is spelling out what he means by religion, draws heavily on the wisdom literature, particularly on Proverbs.[95] He even comments on the cultural context that gave rise to the wisdom literature of ancient Israel: "A time some thousand years before Christ, the golden age of Israel, is the date to which . . . the Book of Proverbs belong[s]. This is the time in which the sense of the necessary connection between righteousness and happiness appears with its full simplicity and force."[96] On the basis of this culture Arnold forms his view of the Bible as a whole. It is the emphasis on right living and wisdom as the transcendent goal of human striving that in Proverbs appeals most to him, and he uses it to interpret the Bible generally. The teaching of Jesus adds an important ingredient, however, because Jesus reveals a secret wisdom that is both profoundly true and apparently contradictory, namely, that one can live more fully when one is released from the tendency to live for oneself and out of self-interest. This secret wisdom points to the transcendent as the "*not ourselves* by which we get the sense for righteousness, and whence we find the help to *do right*."[97]

The Bible can be incorporated in the wider textuality and reading that Arnold means by culture because the Bible, when interpreted in relation to wisdom, can itself be read as literature. It is not science, and it is not valuable for the information that it gives. The information and theology of the Bible are poetry, language, that has been "*thrown out* at the immense reality not fully or half grasped by the writers, but, even thus, able to affect us with indescribable force."[98]

All of this—the analysis of deficiencies and dangers in the present culture, the definition of what culture should be and how the critic is to go about fostering it, and the nature and function of religion—are all background to or stages toward the definition of poetry, or literature, as a steadying, upward-pointing, transhistorical, synthesizing, concentrating, and divinely oriented product of the human spirit. Reading poetry does for culture what reading the Bible once did, but in order so to be read poetry must be excellent. And here again the critic comes in. The critic, by being primarily neither personal nor parochial in interest and orientation, must discover and determine in poetry what belongs to the truly excellent. That can be done not by defining excellence but by having in mind, particularly in the form of short quotations, touchstones by which poetry now being written is compared. The excellence of poetry pertains both to its style and content; both must be marked by truth and seriousness. Indeed, what grants poetry its excellence and exemplary power is that it points beyond itself to a perfection that cannot be articulated but that draws culture upward with a power that is irresistible. Reading literature, then, has a spiritual, even salvific, consequence for culture.

Twentieth-century forms of the moves epitomized by Coleridge and Arnold to read poetry as scripture are incorporated in the New Criticism. It is a practice that derives finally from biblical wisdom, particularly the aspect of wisdom that directs the reader's attention to wisdom itself as a future-oriented, semitranscendent lure that humans ought to pursue even though they cannot fully attain it. It is also supported by discrediting history as not a scripture to be read but a force that threatens culture's moral cohesion and ideal goals. Reading poetry as scripture is closely tied to the increasing difficulty and eventual demise of reading history and nature as scripture. Already in Coleridge but especially in Arnold and all their seed down to recent times, reading literature plays a crucial cultural role by granting access to the unity, vision, and moral direction of a culture that transcends and even defies the alien forces of nature and history.

It is important to emphasize the cultural role imputed to literature and criticism by this tradition from Coleridge and Arnold down through Leavis,

Eliot, and the American New Critics, because such an emphasis offsets how that tradition is construed by many who are suspicious of it. Raymond Williams, Terry Eagleton, Frank Lentricchia, and others have contended that this tradition defined literature in such a transcendent way in order not only to devalue the material sources and supports of literature, particularly labor, but also to validate a ruling class that needed to justify its social position by associating itself with something high or spiritual. I think that this analysis, while not invalid, is incomplete. The cultural practice of reading literature must also be accounted for by its relation in the modern period to reading texts other than the Bible as scripture. The increasing difficulty of reading nature and history as scripture and the increasing need for the third component of wisdom, namely, a transcendent and spiritual lure, created an increased cultural role for reading literature as a practice that would unify people and direct, in a moral or spiritual sense, culture's upward movement.

The New Critics, then, are not merely pressing a political agenda. When, relying heavily on Coleridge and Arnold, I. A. Richards calls the arts "our storehouse of recorded values" because the arts "record the most important judgments we possess as to the value of experience," he speaks as a sapiential theologian.[99] When Cleanth Brooks, drawing heavily on Kant and Arnold, defines poetry primarily in terms of its universality, what he means is that poetry indicates the normative in human life, that toward which people should aspire. Poetry is not about anything less than "man himself."[100] And when W. K. Wimsatt says that poetry must be severed from its historical ties, he does so in order to indicate poetry's upward or transcendent effect. The point is to follow, indeed, to read as a way of following. Because poetry is the text of wisdom, reading it directs one to the transcendent.[101] Although political and even class interests may have marked their ambitious project, the New Critics continued a complex cultural tradition, designating texts that, when read as scripture, would grant access to spiritual realities and moral certainties.

Postmodernist attacks on this tradition and its last representatives should not obscure the fact that modernism was a culture based on theories of textuality and on practices of reading texts as scripture. While theories of textuality return with postmodernism, cultural practices of reading texts as scripture do not, and this failure or lack creates confusion. One cannot but ask what happens to a culture when the practice of reading texts as scripture is lost altogether. Postmodernist culture, defined as the consequence of no longer reading nature, history, and literature as scripture, has no resources in itself to take up the question of "scripture" as a category in textual theory or to revive the kind of reading appropriate to it. Consequently, postmodernism must be examined as deprived of the cultural practice of reading a text as scripture, so that the consequences of this lack will begin to appear. In the next chapter postmodernism, therefore, is described as a series of stages, each one trying to address lacks in the preceding stage but all revealing deficiencies that look beyond to and prepare for the faint return of reading scripture as a cultural practice.

CHAPTER THREE

POSTMODERNITY
*Not Reading Anything At All
As Though It Were Scripture*

"Postmodernism" names a culture that first of all restores textuality and reading to their former but forgotten centrality. Textuality becomes synonymous with culture, and reading becomes a defining cultural practice. Second, it names a culture that, while restoring the centrality of textuality and reading, neglects to include reading texts as scripture. Consequently, reading in this culture becomes an occasion for the reader to project power and significance onto texts by means of design and use. The principal result is not only to shift authority from text to reader but also to remove from the cultural practice of reading the potential of radically challenging, correcting, or reconstituting the personal, group, or institutional location and identity of the reader. The failure of the culture, in its reappropriation of textuality and reading as culturally defining, to include reading texts as scripture has serious consequences.

However, postmodernism's reestablishment of textuality and reading as central to cultural definition and practice must be affirmed. This occurrence was occasioned by the shift in linguistics, marked by the work of Ferdinand de Saussure, from understanding language as secondary, derivative, and referential to understanding language as primary and as generating significance first of all by means of the contrary relations of linguistic units to one another. This linguistic turn was accompanied by the textualization of culture, which subverted the primacy of presence and present time by an emphasis on future and past. This shift was occasioned by the work of Martin Heidegger, and the identification of past and future as textual, and of texts as that to which reference can be made, was accomplished by Jacques Derrida.

By failing to add reading texts as scripture to the reestablishment of textuality and reading, the culture ends up with notions of reading that are consistent with attitudes that arose in the modern period when textuality and reading waned as culturally defining. Notions of reading in postmodernist culture grant power to the reader and subject material to reader interests. The force and significance of reading are determined by the reader's appropriation and use. It is this feature of postmodernist culture that reveals its continuity with and dependence upon modernism.

The postmodernist rejection of modernism for approaching nature, history, and literature not as texts but the loci of something pre- or nontextual, something more certain and enduring than language, did not retrieve the textual status of nature, history, and literature so much as it continued to detextualize the reader and to grant the reader an unprecedented authority to determine the significance and power of texts. The cultural confusion that this shift creates arises from lack of agreement on how interests and assumptions held and prosecuted by the reader and the uses to which the reader puts texts are to be evaluated and, if found objectionable, resisted or sanctioned. Postmodernism provides little indication of what kind of practice would throw the reader—individual, group, or institution—and the reader's use of texts radically into question.

This situation creates what I call a first phase, or stage, in postmodernity. It is marked by irreverence, a ludic style, and an inventiveness, especially combinatorial, toward texts and their applications. This first stage of postmodernism, although it in many ways can be viewed positively, carries consequences that threaten the viability of culture because it contains provisions neither for stabilization nor for raising moral questions, particularly regarding the reader and reading. In discussing this first phase or stage of postmodernism, then, I point out lacks and cracks that jeopardize the culture's viability. This moves the postmodernist narrative toward a second stage, or phase, one marked by attempts to describe inherently stabilizing and determining factors in the culture and to take radical exception to assumptions characteristic of the first phase. While there is much to be gained from and affirmed in these descriptions, they point beyond themselves to the next stage of the narrative because they fail adequately to address the lack, shared with the first stage, of ways to question the reader. The third stage musters some attempts at postmodernist ethics, at providing ways of morally interrogating the present situation, including the position of the reader.

I

The first stage of postmodernism, arising from emphases derived primarily from Nietzsche, is marked by decentering, ludic incoherence, and unimpeded eclecticism and antinomianism. Theories of textuality are folded completely into the dynamics of instability. Linda Hutcheon, in her *Poetics of Postmodernism*, refers to the attitude of readers toward texts characteristic of this ethos as parodic—self-consciously eclectic, constructive, and irreverent.[1] She calls the poetics of postmodernism one of "both/and" rather than "either/or."[2] Yoking contraries, standing above differences, and celebrating incoherence, postmodernism indicates more than a mood or style; it posits choosing, using, and combining as detached from or transcendent over occasions, situations, and materials. Robert Venturi not only wants to affirm the architecture of Las Vegas; he wants to learn from it because it "*includes.*"[3] That is, he takes it as a model of collective irreverence and inventiveness and, in so doing, positions its designers above the textual locations of the themes parodied, juxtaposed, or combined.

This first stage goes a long way in accounting for the popularity of postmodernism. Postmodernism is a household word because this ethos is contagious and upbeat; it calls for a release from forms of foundationalism that implied restraint, appropriate use, or proper place. The contingency now imputed to every position has had the beneficial consequence of opening society, redressing wrongs, and constructing new personal and group identities.[4] Chris Weedon, for example, in her *Feminist Practice and Poststructuralist Theory*, points out that feminist theories and practices would not have gone so far and achieved so much without this ethos. The cultural context created by postmodernism frees the question of gender from its putative grounding and allows gender identity to be open to change, variety, and reconstruction.[5] In a parallel vein theorists of the language of race have been able to free the question of race from its supposed ontological grounding and, as Henry Louis Gates Jr. has done, establish it as a trope subject to social and political uses.[6] Anthony Appiah finds it more helpful to distinguish between societies according to the relative importance of racial distinctions in their texts than to distinguish between races.[7] Identities and locations, once thought of as "natural" or proper, are now recognized as constructed and assigned. Consequently, postmodernism has had liberating, leavening, and exhilarating cultural consequences, and I would not want to return to the old certainties and to all that they supported even if we could.

However, postmodernist reading practices are also culturally inadequate, and lacks and cracks have become increasingly clear. First, these cultural practices disregard the restraints imposed on bits of texts by their larger textual residences. The practice assumes a too easily abstractable and variable quality to textual parts. It is as though the texts that constitute a "culture" or "tradition" are now bits housed in a bin, or grab bag, into which people can reach in order to construct whatever combinations they will. Materials and former practices are too easily assumed to be detachable from their contexts and consequences. But as theorists of gender and race have realized, to free something from its putative ontological status does not mean that its force and tenacity are subverted. Just because a "fact," as Richard Rorty points out, is merely an honorific for what we agree on, this does not mean that "facts," so redefined, can be abstracted, played with, or taken lightly.

The second problem that arises from this phase of postmodernism is that intellectual and aesthetic interests are superseded by social and political forces and their dynamics. Few would contest Frank Lentricchia's statement, "[C]ritical rhetoric which isolates the aesthetic from our political and social lives has run its course."[8] A prominent mark of postmodernist discourses is their self-conscious involvement in political, economic, and social questions and struggles, in alignments with and against structures of power. But when intellectual, aesthetic, and moral factors are determined by political and economic interests, such interests are no longer related to direction, correction, and critique. This has two consequences. The first is that intellectual and aesthetic interests get carried along by political and economic forces they are unable to question. For example, one often sees in postmodernist discourses a distressing ambivalence toward or even a tacit complicity with the culture of late capitalism that, as Scott Lash and John Urry point out, should be defined not only in terms of economics but also as a culture that elevates image over content, performance over meaning, or duplication over particularity.[9] Postmodernism, by imputing primacy to power and a secondary and even derivative role to culture, complies with economic and political interests it is helpless to question. Take architecture, for example, since it provides the context for the sharpest articulations of postmodernist attitudes. As Linda Hutcheon points out, architecture is heavily dependent on and consequently indebted to its economic and political sponsors even while it may be irreverent toward them. Deprived of critical power, intellectual and aesthetic interests are not liberated but are rendered vulnerable to manipulation by concentrations of power. Second, by separation from intellectual and aesthetic interests, political, social, and economic powers emerge as nontextual realities. This unfortunate process is abetted so readily by postmodernist theorists because of their commitments to the power of the reader over texts.

A third problem distressing this phase of postmodernism arises from the contrary estimations it carries regarding agency and the self. On the one hand, there is a thorough deconstruction of the self as either an essentialist fiction or as a product of bourgeois ideology and, on the other, an attribution to the self of uninhibited world-construction. First, the self is construed as the product of social, political, and economic forces, and the choices available to people are described as predetermined and sharply delimited by those systems and forces. The modern myth of the self is exposed as imputing ontological qualities to a political and economic construct. In a more philosophical attack on the modern doctrine of the self, Jacques Derrida deconstructs the concept of the self present to itself as a point of origination, and he replaces it with an understanding of subjects as uncentered and unsteady. However, along with this attack on the originating position of the self, Derrida also grants to the self a remarkable capacity for world-construction. This arises from his discussion of the need for textual centers even though such centers are not predetermined. Centers are always functional, but they are unavoidable. "I believe," he says, "that the center as a function is absolutely indispensable."[10] A person cannot be everywhere in the field of writing, and a person is not somewhere randomly. But the indispensable center becomes a consequence of choice. Location on the textual field arises from free decision, and there is no provision in this argument for textualizing choice, since that would position choice within the problem that the argument for choice is launched to solve. This means that the choice of center inhabits present time. This is a remarkable exception within an otherwise consistent theory, and it occurs at an absolutely crucial juncture, namely, the point of world-constitution. By treating the center as functional, Derrida imputes to particular acts of choosing an originating transcendence over the textual "waters," acts that make a world-constituting choice before entering its textual determinations. I point out this remarkable moment in Derrida's theory not in order to discredit the theory but to reveal its uncertainty about the self. One finds postmodernist discourses distressed by a vacillation between notions of the self as absorbed and determined by social and cultural systems and of the self remarkably free to constitute its own identity and its own world. This vacillation produces wide mood swings in the culture, from the assumption that one has no chance to establish particularity in the face of enormously determining social forces to its contrary, imagining oneself as free to construct any life one may choose.

A fourth problem in postmodern discourses arises from a separation between the language of fragmentation and the language of totalization. Robert Venturi stresses totalization when he points out that communication dominates architecture and that the message is single and commercial.[11] Richard Harland, in his book *Superstructuralism*, argues that the human now has been absorbed by semiotic systems.[12] Fredric Jameson refers to a cultural system and world economy that not only are all-encompassing but, by virtue of inclusiveness and size, are unrepresentable.[13] And Jean Baudrillard's *America* is a description of our society as a single, all-inclusively plastic, mechanical, and electronic space.[14] But just as (perhaps even more) prevalent and insistent in the discourses of postmodernity is the language of fragmentation. Jean-François Lyotard announces the death of the meta-narrative and the rise of societies agonistically constituted of discordant interests.[15] Fractionalization, loose ends, and indeterminacy are defining themes of these discourses. Edith Wyschogrod, for example, not only uses the characteristic of fragmentation as one of her six defining descriptions of postmodernist discourses, she also uses it as a determining feature of her entire project.[16] The question exposed by the contradictory positions of postmodernist theorists is how to bring together these now disjoined emphases of fragmentation and totalization. The two categories are social variations of the categories of particulars and universals that mark discourse itself. A disconnection between them threatens predication and significance. While there will always be a tension between the two or a shift in a culture from an emphasis now on one to an emphasis now on the other, a separation of the two in the same culture cannot be productive of meaning and exacerbates an already uncritical participation in, or at least vulnerability to, the dynamics and structures of political and economic power.

A final problem in postmodernist discourses is created by the role taken within them by the language of space or place. This is no small matter, for the language of space dominates these discourses. Fredric Jameson remarks, "I think it is at least empirically arguable that our daily life, our psychic experience, our cultural languages, are today dominated by categories of space rather than by categories of time, as in the preceding period of high modernism proper."[17] One reason for this dominating role of the language of space may be the importance of architecture as a site for articulating the distinction between postmodernism and modernism. Another reason may be the authority within these discourses of social and economic analyses and models, which tend to be spatial and synchronic. So, for example, Pierre Bourdieu in *Distinction* offers an analysis of taste in contemporary French culture not, as with Hans-Georg Gadamer, in terms of history and tradition but, rather, in terms of class-specific locations.[18] Ernesto Laclau and Chantal Mouffe, in their *Hegemony and Socialist Strategy*, are given over almost wholly to spatial language because they want to avoid, with their post-Marxist project, the teleologies implicit in the language of time. Lyotard and Foucault stress the language of place and space because for them institutions validate and stabilize the powers of discourses. But while the language of place and space dominates these discourses, it is often abstract or formal, shaping the discourses, but not itself discursively or textually located or particularized. This may be due, perhaps more than to anything else, to the suspicion of narrative in these discourses. So, for example, Robert Venturi can be so celebrative of the architecture of Las Vegas because he is interested in spaces abstractly considered and not in relation to the kind of setting they provide for the narratives of people and their behavior, of those who financed these constructions for certain ends and those who spend their time and livelihood there. What economic and psychological intentions and consequences are attached to designing buildings in which people inhabiting them become unaware of the passage of time? Unnarrativized, free-floating spatial language, rather than exceptional, is typical of postmodernist discourses, and it carries unmistakable signs of manipulation.

These five problems arise in the first stage of postmodernism and bring about or set the terms for a second stage. In this next stage, reading as a cultural practice is granted more stability. However, attempts to address the lacks and ambiguities in the first stage fall short by not providing any way in which the reader's position or the institutions or systems in which the reader is located can be called into question.

II

Barbara Herrnstein Smith provides a good example of an attempt to address the aporias of postmodernism. Although her work is most widely known for its attack on modernist assumptions of inherent significance and value, she moves from those attacks to a theory of how values are determined and stabilized in a culture. While she addresses primarily the question of determining literary value, Smith does not limit her position to judgments of this kind alone. She houses her theory of literary evaluation in a comprehensive account of how the importance, validity, and goodness of things, events, and ideas are determined. Her treatment of judgment is inclusive of kinds and levels.[19]

While she attacks claims that judgments of value are based on intrinsic and objective qualities, she rejects the notion that value judgments are subjective or matters of whim and caprice. She does this by deploying a social-economic model for explaining how values are determined, a model that also keeps value from arising from anything exceptional to the system. The principal metaphors that she uses to describe this system are economic, and she places the question of value in a theory of exchange; society is a marketplace where values are exchanged by means of a system in which the terms of exchange are provided by the notion of value (or truth or goodness) itself.[20]

Having deployed this context for value judgments, Smith goes on to resist the notion that value judgments form a discrete set of acts. Value judgments are inextricably related to a complex of interests and intentions. This integration of all value judgments of whatever kind into the ongoing dynamics and complexities of economically described social interactions prevents values from assuming some separate position above or apart from the contaminations of ordinary activities or constituting a "sacred" realm above or apart from social dynamics and over which only a certain group of "priests" have jurisdiction.[21]

This allows her to make a third point, namely, that all judgments, since they are inseparable from systems of social interaction, are interested and instrumental. There is no such thing for her as a disinterested act, thought, or judgment. Every value judgment is made in relation to something else; something is good *for* or *as* something.[22] This is not to say that all value judgments are of equal importance; the social systems that require and enable value judgments incorporate criteria by which some value judgments are considered to be more valuable than others. But because not all value judgments are on the same level, one should not conclude that some are made by dynamics that differ from others.[23]

Although some decisions regarding value, such as acts of charity, seem to be disinterested, Smith insists that charitable acts are based on the same exchange system as are those recognizably self-serving. The values operative are simply different. So, too, the decision of a person or group to forgo its own interests for the sake of the society as a whole arises when the concord or preservation of society has become important to the person or group.[24] Finally, Smith takes up the case of Georges Bataille, who identifies profligate expenditure, loss without hope or even desire for return, as a basic human need. Smith argues that Bataille, by making loss desirable, turns loss into a value one can obtain only by giving up everything.[25] All value judgments belong to an economy in which people participate in social transactions with an aim to achieve ends or acquire rewards that they value.

Smith, while she relativizes and destabilizes values, imputes stability and regularity to the determination and exchange of values. While value does not have objective standing as inhering in certain things or events, the standards regulating the exchange of values and the negotiations among values are objective in the sense that they have social, political, and economic standing and support. Individuals, groups, and institutions participate in those standards because all are primarily social. They are all incorporated within an inclusive membrane, or field, of interactions that constitute Smith's "market." She states her position clearly and succinctly when she says, "All value is radically contingent, being neither a fixed attribute, an inherent quality, or an objective property of things but, rather, an effect of multiple, continuously changing, and continuously interacting variables or, to put this another way, the product of the dynamics of a system, specifically an *economic* system."[26] Smith does not relieve society of this determining role by assigning to smaller communities within the social system some responsibilities for establishing values in their own way. While "*each of us* is a member of many, shifting communities, each of which establishes, for *each* of its members, multiple social identities, multiple principles of identification with other people, and, accordingly, a collage or grab-bag of allegiances, beliefs, and sets of motives," these smaller communities do not have their own ways of establishing value, and those who hold to such theories of communal particularity and identity invite or prosecute forms of "social-political isolationism" and "neo-objectivism."[27]

The pressures placed on the stabilizing role of the social whole are enormous not only because Smith minimizes the role played by smaller groups within the society but also because individuals themselves lack coherence. Rather than single or constant, selves are systems of "*multiple* economies, each of which . . . may at any point come into more or less radical conflict [with other economies in the system]." Out of such conflicts and interactions we "construct our various versions of our various 'selves' and, as necessary, explain or justify our actions, goals and beliefs."[28] Since individuals and groups cannot be exempt from the dynamics of value determination, appropriation, and exchange, tremendous value is placed by her theory on the social "marketplace" and the economic dynamics that determine all. They constitute what all participants in the social system share. Individuals cannot stand apart from the system to criticize it in the name of some value absent from the system.[29] While the chief value is the social system whereby or within which all values are determined, it is not a value with meaning and direction.[30] In other words, it and its value are not textual.

While I admire Smith's attempt to move beyond the first stage of post-modernism by accounting for the constraints and determinations of value in human judgments and interactions, I have several reservations about the adequacy of her model. The first has to do with the strong endorsement of society and its economically described dynamics that her position carries. Her theory implies an approbation of society and its marketlike dynamics that seems unqualified, a passivity toward and acceptance of social economy that lack, as a counterweight, reasons for such trust and approval. If the society and its market dynamics are what establish value, then the chief value is that society. However, since there is no place from which to examine that society and nothing upon which to argue for its value, its value must be taken on faith. In addition, it is not clear where a society derives its value, since it is not itself a part of some cosmic market. A society seems to have its value intrinsically and to have it in ways that cannot be challenged. Finally, since only value within a society and not society itself is subject to change, society, despite all the emphasis on history and interactions in her work, is atemporal.

Second, she indicates that a society also needs continuity and concord and that at times this need may be so prominent that people will forgo self-interest for the benefit of the whole, a value that is also, although not in the same way, self-serving. She includes a very interesting account of how and why canons are formed and how and why cultures not only shape their canons but are shaped by them.[31] But it is not clear how this balance or exchange between diversity and individuality on the one hand and continuity and concord on the other is administered. No provision is made for how a society is to recognize that it is getting too much of one and not enough of the other, so as to make the necessary adjustment. Again, the norms for determining when there is too much of one or of the other seem to be intrinsic to the system. This is no small matter. The model she offers depends on at least a rough balance between individual and group interests, and she records shifts in her model from one to the other. But it is not clear where the norm of balance resides, why anyone should heed it, or when and how the "right" balance is achieved.

Third, in her analysis of appeals to acts of charity or in her response to Bataille, she seems to use the category of "value" so loosely that it no longer has meaning. When she calls charity a form of self-interest and total loss a highest gain, one wonders what "economic" meaning "value" and "profit" any longer have. If charity is actually self-interest and loss is actually gain, value no longer is a category with sufficient recognizable force or meaning to indicate a steady or coherent market of exchange. Indeed, one wonders, in this theory of exchange value, whether exchange is more important than value, whether a society of use and exchange is being advocated more than a way of determining values.

Fourth, I believe that the category of functionally noncontingent values to which she makes passing reference needs more fully to be theorized.[32] I wonder, first of all, why they arise only in communities, why the "self," especially with all the diversity Smith locates there, does not, as well, require or produce them. The category of functionally noncontingent values is potentially too important for such minimal treatment. I would say that there are values that function for people and groups noncontingently, that there are values of which people are not aware but upon which they depend, that there are values that people would not consider exchanging, and that there are values that support the process of value exchange. But I would move in that direction in order to identify the "market" as itself textual, as dependent upon functionally noncontingent values that operate and can be read as scripture.

Indeed, textuality is an underdeveloped category in Smith's account. She talks about the formation and role of canons as relatively stable factors in a culture, and more important, she says in passing that "the subject's experiences of an entity are not discrete or, strictly speaking, successive, because recollection and anticipation always overlap perception."[33] But her position requires a more developed theory of textuality in order to account for the trust that people have in the whole, for the particularity and relatively constant role of the meaning of value, and for the mix people tolerate of diversity and agreement or uncertainty and stability. The texts of recollection and anticipation not only condition the perceptions of individuals, they also condition groups and societies. Smith seems to be describing not a specific, textually formed society but societies as they actually are in some pre- or nontextual state. Consequently, she offers not so much a description of what, say, *our* society and we as participants in it are like, a situation that we could, perhaps, deplore and want to alter. Rather, this is how societies and people in them operate, and the deconstructive part of her work serves to expose how things really *are*. Moreover, her description suggests not only that this situation must be acknowledged and accepted, since there is no way of changing it, but also that it ought to be accepted because it is basically acceptable, that is, good. This places Smith in a position roughly analogous to historicists who want the course of history to be accepted and affirmed as basically good because they are people who have done well by way of that history. So, one could say that the market and profit motive would be deployed as a descriptive ontology only by a person or group that has done quite well by means of them, since a situation in which they have prospered is thereby being reinforced and confirmed.

While Stanley Fish agrees with much in Smith, he departs from her by turning in a direction that she discredits, namely, toward the stabilizing roles for determining value that are played by communities within the society. This move gives Fish's position more focus and clarity, since it is more partial. But these qualities also weaken the potential adequacy of his position, since they raise the question whether a description of value determination in one community can be applied to others or to the whole.

I should point out at the outset that Fish is as anti-objectivist as Smith. He is well known as a reader-response theorist of the most thorough kind. For example, he not only says that the meaning of a text is determined by the reading of it, he also says that what is read is constructed by the reader, that there is not even, before the operations of readers' interests, an existing text. Anything we read or perceive, and he uses the two terms interchangeably, we make into objects to be read and perceived: "[P]erception (and reading is an instance of perception) always occurs within a set of assumptions that preconstrains what could possibly be perceived (or heard, or tasted, or touched)." Along with texts, of course, kinds of texts are also constructed by readers; hence, for example, "literature" is "a conventional category, the content and scope of which is continually a matter of debate and adjudication between historically conditioned agents."[34] Reading, as a practice that determines an object and its meaning, gives "texts their shape, making them rather than, as is usually assumed, arising from them."[35] Or again, "In my model . . . meanings are not extracted but made and made not by encoded forms but by interpretive strategies that call forms into being." And this is so in all cases: "The truth is not a matter of a special relationship it bears to the world (the world does not impose it on us) but of a special relationship it bears to its users."[36] Fish's theory of reading, consequently, reemphasizes and even increases the power attributed to the reader in what

I call the first stage of postmodernism. For Fish, reading is an act by which the text and the reading of it are subsumed wholly under and appropriated by the "world" of the reader.

Fish, however, like Smith, does not want his anti-objectivism to force him into subjectivism. It is not the case, he argues, that because interpretation is not constrained by what is "there," "interpreters, in the absence of such constraints, are free to read into a text whatever they like."[37] Indeed, for Fish, as perhaps also for Smith, this second point, anti-subjectivism, is the more important one to make, and it fuels much of his opposition to the putative freedom in reading implied or claimed by postmodernism in its first stage. Fish, like Smith, counters notions that make reading a freewheeling and unrestrained cultural practice. For Smith, "anything goes" is countered by the value intrinsic to a social system in which not everything pays. Fish counters the unrestrained or undetermined interpretive situation by means of a social model, too, but his model is more communal. A reader is never wholly free, because "perception is always conventional (and therefore readers are never free)."[38] There is no escape from such determinations. "What the critical theorists [what I have called postmodernists of the first stage] call liberation or emancipation is nothing more (or less) than the passing from one structure of constraint to another, a passing that will always be attended by . . . possibilities that will be no less (or more) constrained than those that have been left behind."[39] Indeed, his philosophical anthropology is anti-individualistic: "In short, to the list of made or constructed objects we must add ourselves, for we no less than the poems and assignments we see are the products of social and cultural patterns of thought."[40] The constraints placed on a person that determine what that person will take to be an object worthy of attention, how that person constructs the object, and how that person interprets it are not single. Persons participate in many communities, with the result that persons will attend to, construct, and interpret many differing objects or will attend, construct, and interpret the same object in more or less differing ways as that person moves from circle to circle.[41]

Fish's principal designation for these determinations is "communities of interpretation." His chief examples are professions, particularly the legal and literary professions. This is perhaps the most well-known aspect of his position, and I shall be brief about it. Interpretive communities are the authoritatively determining situations in which texts are identified as worthy of attention, constituted, and interpreted, and the legal and literary professions are the clearest and most exemplary instances of what is more generally true of the communally determined character of human perceptions and interpretations. The professions are the means by which Fish introduces a stabilizing and even authoritative factor to counteract the freewheeling consequences or assumptions that would otherwise follow from postmodernism's first phase. Indeed, for Fish, postmodernism's supposed freedom is only an illusion, for reading always is and always has been constrained. So strong is his emphasis on the stabilizing consequences of communities, epitomized by professions, that Fish posits a culture that, even though it may now have antifoundationalist understandings, resembles in every other way foundationalist cultures: "But anti-foundationalist thought deprives us of nothing; all it offers is an alternative account of how the certainties that will still grip us when we are persuaded to it came to be in place."[42]

Not only does Fish differ from Smith in his stress on particular communities, exemplified by professions, in countering with their determinations the indeterminacy and possible whimsicality of reading, he also differs from her by a stress on force and politics in place of her models of free-market exchange. Fish employs the category of force in a number of ways. At one level it is consistent with his social model; he describes the activities of professions as attempts by people and parties to alter the beliefs of others. This is done not by evidence, since "evidence" is what people are persuaded to accept as evidence, but by force, that is, by influence, notably by rhetorical strategies but by other means as well.[43] He says, for example, "[F]orce is the sole determinant of outcomes, but the sting is removed from this conclusion when force is understood not as 'pure' or 'mere' force (phenomena never encountered) but as the urging (perhaps in the softest terms) of some point of view, of some vision of the world complete with purposes, goals, standards, reasons—in short, with everything to which force is usually opposed in the name of principle." Fish seems to take delight in pointing out that intellectuals, while they want to deny the fact, are always in the business of using force, which is simply "a (pejorative) name for the thrust or assertion of some point of view." In addition, Fish emphasizes force to turn attention to the neglected role of rhetoric in academic and professional life. He attacks the conventions of academic life and the philosophical assumptions that sponsor it for their aversion to rhetoric or their treatment of it as the dressing of discourse. But for the "*homo rhetoricus* rhetoric is *both* form and content, the manner of presentation and what is presented."[44] Indeed, Fish sees postmodernism largely as the rehabilitation of rhetoric and the recognition of its cultural position and consequences. Finally, Fish emphasizes force in more blatantly political terms. His analysis of the professions and those who speak with authority in them and his attack on the notion of free speech in the name of the limitations of speech always present and always politically determined are only two instances of his readiness to invoke political power as a way of determining what is allowed, taken seriously, judged beneficial, or awarded praise.[45] Indeed, one of the most crucial (perhaps worrisome) aspects of his work is the way in which power as intellectual persuasion and power as political force are not distinguished from one another.

The third crucial point to Fish's position, from which again he differs from Smith and most of his colleagues in the postmodernist reconstructive enterprise, is his emphasis on belief. Values are not so much, as with Smith, what a person gains and possesses as what possess a person, not so much what a person negotiates as what enable a person to negotiate and what negotiate the person. I would say that his theory of beliefs as determinative of practice and theory, like Smith's notion of functionally noncontingent values, constitutes a lasting contribution to the second stage, or phase, of postmodernist discourse. Fish is insistent in his theory of the status and role of beliefs: "It is in the name of personally held (in fact they are doing the holding) norms and values that the individual acts and argues, and he does so with the full confidence that attends belief."[46] Beliefs are unavoidable for Fish: "It is thus a condition of human life always to be operating as an extension of beliefs and assumptions that are historically contingent, and yet to be holding these beliefs and assumptions with an absoluteness that is the necessary consequence of the absoluteness with which they hold—inform, shape, constitute—us."[47] Knowledge, experience, evidence—these do not create belief; belief always antedates them: "Beliefs are not what you think *about* but what you think *with*, and it is within the space provided by their articulations that mental activity—including the activity of theorizing—goes on. Theories are something you can have . . . ; beliefs have *you*, in the sense that there can be no distance between them and the acts they enable." Fish takes what only is hinted at in Smith's category of functionally noncontingent values and enlarges it to an inclusive and determining position. Indeed, Fish is not hesitant to echo traditional theological terms of the relation of faith to understanding: he says, "[R]easons are like the reasons given in the catechism; they are reasons for your faith, and they are also reasons that derive from your faith in a circular but not vicious relationship."[48] Even when a person knows that his or her beliefs are local and partial that person "will nevertheless experience those convictions as universally, not locally, true."[49]

These three emphases of Fish—interpretive communities, rhetorical and political force, and the enabling and directing role of belief in human practices—give his position a resonance and complexity that Smith's more general, economic model lacks. He also takes up the question of temporality, which, as I noted, is underdeveloped in Smith. Fish calls interpretive communities, which, remember, are exemplified in professions, not instruments of preservation and protection but engines of change. He says, "[S]ince an interpretive community is an engine of change, there is no status quo to protect, for its operations are inseparable from the transformation of both its assumptions and interests; and since the change that is inevitable is also orderly—constrained by evidentiary procedures and tacit understandings that at once enable change and are changed by what they enable—license and willful irresponsibility are never possibilities."[50] Although Fish's position, by including an account of belief and of temporality, is more adequate than Smith's, it leaves lacks and creates problems that call for response.

First, Fish ontologizes professional communities. Not only does he posit them as exemplary, he also locates within them as constitutive of their very existence the resolution of those contraries that have always dogged the philosophy of time, namely, the relation in temporality of change to constancy. He simply tucks into the category of "interpretive community" the full responsibility, which he takes on trust, of establishing the right relations between one another of such contraries as constancy and change, stability and alteration, unity and diversity. It is analogous to Smith's incorporation within the dynamics of society the crucial determination, for its very existence, of how individual and group interests and needs are to be balanced. The principal basis Fish provides for this move is the human mind itself as an engine of change, and he includes under that metaphor social communities "by extension."[51] This attribution of balance or right mixture of contraries to the already existing system that Fish, like Smith, makes is an arresting form of "realized eschatology." Few would place so much trust in institutions, to use another name for "communities," because institutions are always in need of restraint and reform both from within and from without. To ontologize an institution or, in Smith's case, a social system is to exempt it from critique.

It will not do for Fish to charge those who call communities or institutions and society more generally into question "essentialists" or "idealists," because Fish has simply troweled his essences and ideals into the existing situation. There are no significant remainders, because he, like Smith, suffers no—or very little—dissonance between his values and the constitution and operation of institutions of which he is a part. Like Smith, Fish avoids the charge of being an idealist, because the values to which he subscribes are already realized in the institutions where he presides. Fish does not question the professions, because they are as they should be, not because he has no ideals. The judgment that "nothing is lacking" does not compare with the judgment that "something is lacking" as nonidealist to idealist but as realized to prophetic eschatology.

This is no small matter. With the thrust given his theory by the unlocated and undifferentiated use of the category of "force," by the advocacy of the literary profession as an exemplary social community, and by virtue of his own position of authority in that profession, one could say that it does not serve his political interests to detach values from their present incarnation in those constructions and arrangements. In other words, Fish's position, with all of its richly helpful ingredients, finally comes down to voice-warranting. Not only does his theory support his professional, political position, but it also is a theory that makes the use of theory for such support legitimate.

While I do not accept some aspects of his theory—that interpretive communities are extensions of mind and its capacity to effect orderly change, that professional communities are exemplary of all social systems, and that there need be nothing within or outside a community that would call its procedures, values, and goals radically into question—I have high regard for his analysis of the position and role of belief. His doctrine of belief, however, is inadequate because he locates beliefs primarily as implicit in the interpretive acts of people in communities. He does this in order not to ascribe textuality to beliefs. To locate beliefs in texts would be to objectify them, and this would undermine the indeterminacy of texts upon which his whole theory is built and which his doctrine of beliefs is deployed to balance. To sharpen the point, recognizing the textuality of beliefs would subvert the power that he wants not so much the professions as their leaders, among whom he is justified to count himself, to retain. But lodging the beliefs of the professions in the performance of those leaders who act within them as "forces" is not only to de-textualize the culture of professions but also to deprive them of any basis for self-critique.

III

The third, or ethical, stage in the narrative of postmodernism arises because the status and role of systems and communities for determining value and significance in the second stage cannot, because they are basically nontextual, be themselves brought into question. Smith and Fish, for example, provide no possibility of criticizing the systems and communities they posit and affirm. There seems to be no option but to accept them. Indeed, everyone is in a system or community that cannot be interrogated, because that interrogation is part of the system or community. Acceptance of or acquiescence to these systems may not trouble people who have done well within them, but a theory of acceptance that does not provide for its own interrogation is a simple act of identity- or voice-warranting.

Where these positions err is in the assumption that the principal, if not exclusive, problem with postmodernism's first stage is lack of coherence, stability, and continuity. But the problem is as much how to allow one's self, group, institution or even system to be questioned. The third, or ethical, stage of postmodernism tries to compensate this lack and to do so without reintroducing discredited notions of transcendence. I present three recent attempts to locate some basis for the ethical interrogation of society or culture and to avoid returning to the absolutist or objectivist notions that mark the status and role of ethical norms in modern thought. I move from an example I find least successful to two I find more productive in their engagement with this very urgent and difficult problem. But I have questions about the more successful attempts, too, and thereby direct the narrative toward practices, described in the work of Maurice Blanchot and Julia Kristeva, that suggest the faint return of reading texts as scripture.

The first and least successful example of this third, ethical stage in postmodernism is provided by Steven Connor's *Theory and Cultural Value*. Connor takes his position both with and against Barbara Herrnstein Smith. He objects to her model because it fails to provide norms for making systemwide judgments, but he does not want to return to the modernist position that Smith discredits. He also attacks her position by claiming that a market metaphor for describing how values are determined and exchanged flattens or homogenizes all values, so that Smith ends up with an uninterestingly level field of values shaped by and for a single market economy. In addition to this leveling effect on the variety of values in human society, Smith, he argues, cannot give an adequate account of the differing value systems of various people. He claims that for her, finally, there is no way to avoid interpreting all values as mere preferences, and, when this occurs, a noticeable disparity arises between her account of values and the actual role of values in the lives of at least some people. Finally, he believes that Smith does not give an account of the implicit value that she places on a society that is constituted of diversity, indeed, that fosters unlimited diversity. Although he does not say it, he seems to see a polarization in her work between a single, simplistic or even reductive theory of value, on the one hand, and, on the other, an affirmation of extreme social diversity, making the two aggravate and depend upon one another.

Connor sees the lack in the current situation principally as the need to bring together again values that have been polarized. He discusses an array of postmodernists in order to display how they allow values to fall into contradictory relations to one another, values that, while differing, need to be brought together or held in tension. For example, he discusses the contradictory positions taken on the question of pleasure, whether it is to be affirmed or denied. He displays the alternatives as quite extreme on both sides: the disdain for pleasure because pleasure is determined either by capitalist interests or by male understandings of pleasure; and the affirmation of pleasure, of the carnival spirit and of *jouissance*. Or, again, he contrasts the affirmation of excess in the work of Bataille and the opposite quest for poverty and restraint in Beckett. He locates another polarized situation between Habermas and Lyotard in that one affirms consensus and the other conflict in human discourse. Connor analyzes the work of a number of theorists concerned with the relation of aesthetics to politics, and he sees this as an issue unproductively distressed by the polarizations that have arisen between these two human interests. His discussion of feminist theorists turns on the problems that arise in these discourses from the contrasting emphasis on shared human values, such as justice, and on values determined by and in relation to the particularity of women's interests. And, finally, he discusses the unfortunate severance of alterity in postmodernist discourses from questions of relationship, arguing that the language of the other, of distance and incommensurability, is potentially or actually as violent as its opposite, the language of appropriation and the same.

Connor, in response to these polarizations, posits language itself as the norm and value by which polarizations and the impasses they create can be transcended. He argues that because every discourse is particular, every claim for a systemwide value is corrected by the context in which that claim is made; but just as important, every claim for relativity in values cannot be made without some general or systemwide sense of what is valuable or what determines values, or in the name of what value particular values ought to be protected or preserved.[52] Without going into detail or arguing this point directly, Connor implies that language itself contains systemwide value and that language can and should be recognized as the means by which contraries that have unfortunately and unnecessarily become contradictions can be brought into relation once again. He implies, moreover, that literary discourses have exceptional ethical potential because they call attention to the capacity in language to sustain contraries and to overcome polarizations. Finally, he implies that language, because of this capacity to counter the social trends toward polarization, has a certain transcendent, ethical role to play. Indeed language, unlike other media of exchange, does not subject value to itself or become itself the value but, especially in literary discourses, defers to values that it sustains. This self-effacement of literary language makes it an ethically reliable bearer not only of particular cultural values but of the greater cultural value of keeping contrary values in mutually corrective relations to one another.

While much is commendable in Connor's ethical project, especially the reemphasis on language and textuality, it carries an affirmation of the ethical and cultural authority of literary texts that throws us back into a modernist ethos. The works of James Joyce are particularly affirmed. This puts us back into the position of positing the practice of reading literature as culturally normative, since literature is pointing out how language, which can save us from the dichotomies by which the culture is distressed, moves ahead of us inviting imitation and trust. By trying to move beyond the lacks of postmodernism in its first phase and also beyond the absence of norms in the second phase, Connor seems to revert to reading literature as a modernist normative practice, the tradition, that is, of Coleridge, Arnold, and the New Critics. Indeed, his high estimation of literature due to its ability to contain ambiguities, tensions, and contraries suggests that tradition strongly, and he imputes a transcendence to literary language above the conflicts and polarizations to which history, given its social and political dynamics, is prone. Without the idealist assumptions that upheld that tradition of belief, Connor ends with an unsubstantiated confidence in literature and in the cultural consequences of reading it. Instead of exposing a systemwide norm for making ethical judgments, he has elevated one particular kind of language use as normative and even salvific for the whole.

A second, more convincing attempt at postmodernist ethics, at locating a norm by which social interests, practices, and institutions can be challenged, is offered by Edith Wyschogrod's *Saints and Postmodernism: Revisioning Moral Philosophy*. Wyschogrod isolates the life of the saint as an arresting departure from the currents of contemporary culture, a departure that, if it does not imply some general judgment, calls the adequacy of the culture into question. The singular, which she contends is not homologous to or a segment of the social but marks departure and exception, subverts the completeness and intransigence of the whole.

Aware that ethics and moral theory are stymied because there is no way to secure theory as an imperative for behavior and because there is no common ground on which to mount norms that can be shared, Wyschogrod turns to exceptional actions that arrest attention and for that reason have authority. Positing the force of the singular over the corporate, action over theory, and the body's specificity over moral principles, she points to the radical and excessive desire of the saint for the total well-being of the other as a critical and liberating departure from the determinations and structures of late capitalist culture.

Wyschogrod argues that the life of a saint does not have normativity by embodying moral principles, because the saint frequently departs from morally grounded behavior. Only in retrospect does the life of the saint constitute a moral norm. The moral values of saintly action are embodied in the behavior and must be inferred from it. However, even when the moral values of the saint's actions have been articulated in propositions, they do not become norms; nothing can substitute for the authority of the saintly life, and it has an authority that attracts others to imitate or to follow it. In addition, she argues, the saint's behavior cannot be understood theologically, that is, as behavior arising from the saint's beliefs in the transcendent. Not all saints are mystics, and the saint is one whose interest does not lie outside or beyond the recipient of the saint's care but lies in the object of that care. Finally, she argues that the saint cannot be taken as one who finds pleasure in suffering. While there are some similarities between the interests and behavior of saints and masochists, there are more important differences, particularly that the saint dislikes pain and wants to counter or remove it.

Wyschogrod does not want to limit saintly action to a particular culture. She affirms that there are remarkable family resemblances among the behaviors of saints in differing cultures. And saints appear in the secular narratives of the West as well as in religious hagiography. The force and appeal of saintly behavior appear widely in biography, autobiography, and fiction. She is prepared to hypothesize a human potential for saintly behavior, which accounts for the appeal of the lives of saints and the many ways those lives are read by people. She posits "a rudimentary sensitivity to others" within people, although not all people yield to the lure of saintly behavior.[53] This is not to say that a person who does yield to that lure is actualizing a latent natural potential; the capacity for and shape of saintly behavior are constituted by the activity itself, by saintly practice. Such practices carry authority because people recognize them as counter to prevailing cultural attitudes and social actions; and because they stand out so clearly from the whole, they suggest to others analogous, though perhaps less dramatic, behavior.

In her description of saintly behavior, Wyschogrod concentrates on the dynamics of relation that arise between the saint and the one to whom the saint attends. First, the saint is drawn, by that person's alterity, to stand outside the normal flow of cultural interests and social transactions. This sense of the other is never lost in the saint's actions; the saint does not appropriate the suffering other or deposit him- or herself into the life of the other. The saint is brought into relation with the other and out of relation with cultural directives and social rewards. Wyschogrod calls the basis for the relation between the saint and the object of saintly care "dark diachronicity." What she means by this is the recognition not so much of shared mortality as of time running out. That is, a significant point of relation between people is the fact that the time in which each of us is living is the time that each has left. The force of this time on each of us and the recognition of termination provide the basis of relations between people no matter how different from one another they otherwise may be. The other to whom the saint attends allows the saint to enter his or her own time so understood, and when entered, that time becomes a time of passion and of transformation, of dying but also of revivification.

The principal sign of this shared temporality, to which the saint attends, is the other's face. A face, though singular, can be read, and reading a face need not involve deconstruction because "*it always already bespeaks finitude.*"[54] The face of the other is the point of exit that lures the saint out of cultural conventions, institutional limits, and social abstractions into postures, relations, and actions that have moral power. The ethic of this culturally disruptive and socially destabilizing behavior can only be understood from within; the rules are not external or prior to it. From the outside, it is not possible to tell what it is that motivates the saint, whether altruism or self-interest. The force and validity of saintly behavior must be felt by the body in action.[55]

The possibility of an "ethics," that is, of a generally shared sense of the normative by which society, its institutions, and the behavior society demands and rewards can be challenged, arises from places marked or exposed by occasions of saintly behavior. When Wyschogrod says that "*social theories do not measure altruism but altruism measures social theories,*" I take her to mean that a society can be judged by the degree to which the sites of saintly behavior are noticed and valued.[56] Implied is the argument that a society can be evaluated by the kinds of behaviors that are admired and emulated. To the degree that ruthless self-interest is rewarded and admired, society can be judged as morally deficient because it is inattentive to actuality, to what there is about life that reveals the conventional as derivative and deceptive.

This formulation of a postmodernist ethic generates its power by indicating a path and a discipline by which the determinations of the culture are eluded and an exit from the system of social exchanges is secured. This gives a singularity to the saintly life, and that life becomes a text that allows others, by reading, to exit as well. This last point brings this position very close to what it means to read a text as scripture, but Wyschogrod's project raises questions that, I think, make the alternative toward which this narrative is moving more viable than that which she advocates.

First, Wyschogrod posits the face of the other, the body, and "dark diachronicity" as actualities that have immediate moral force because they lie outside of language. True, she relates the lives of saints to texts, but saintly behavior itself is actualized by the saint's relations to suffering particularity and not to texts. The face of the other is exceptional and therefore arresting to the extent that it is nontextual. This nontextual reality she posits as an exit from the culture, a point that implicitly questions the whole. However, it could be argued that her position is recognizable and forceful because the faces she refers to are textual and thereby recognizable. We are led to notice such faces and to recognize the exceptions that their suffering arrestingly poses, because we have been taught to do so by the texts and iconography of what she calls sainthood. The force of what she says owes everything to those texts. Her attempt to posit an actuality outside of cultural patterns and their determinations leads her to posit something nontextual, as though it were textuality and not the culture that presents the problem. The "reality" to which she points has its status as exception or norm because of texts. Her ethics makes a modernist move—unnecessarily, I think—by locating outside of textuality a foundation or, at least, a leverage point that is posited as crucial to the significance and force of that ethics.

Second, Wyschogrod's ethics, while it appeals to actuality, derives from cultural determinations and conformities. It is by its contrasting relation to dominant cultural patterns that the behavior she describes gains singularity and force. The principal points of her description—the body, "dark diachronicity," and desire for the total well-being of the other—gather their force and authority, their normativity, by means of their opposition to the prevailing and constitutive attitudes and behaviors of the culture. An ethic of exception is produced by the textual field of which it is a part and from which it stands out. In other words, her ethic depends for its force and significance on being exceptional, but it is made exceptional by a culture of abstraction, self-interest, and exchange, that is, by a culture such as ours. Finally, if the nontextual and exceptional are to be made normative, access to them needs more fully to be detailed. There is an unexplained attraction and authority imputed to them. Presumed is a weariness with the cultural and with unexceptional behavior. Presumed as well is the failure of other culturally divergent behaviors to claim the authority of the exceptional and to divert attention away from saints and to themselves. There is so little account of the process of regarding saints because there is little attention given in her position to the cultural practice of reading.

Simon Critchley's *Ethics of Deconstruction: Derrida and Levinas* offers a third attempt to provide norms by which the culture can be challenged in its assumptions and practices. Critchley locates the ethical in deconstruction itself by elaborating the relations and contrasts that exist and can be clarified between Derrida and Levinas. Revealed in their juxtaposition is the possibility of ethics within interstices and in the hesitancy or uncertainty that they represent. Critchley tries to supply an ethical and political supplement to their work that will counteract the tendency that he otherwise sees in postmodernist discourses toward immanentism and totalization, tendencies that I have highlighted in the work of Smith and Fish. Critchley's problem, of course, is how to present an ethic that is designed to keep uncertainty, the unincorporated, and the singular, in their actuality and transcendence, from being domesticated and dissolved in the theory about them. The danger is that in going beyond deconstruction he no longer speaks within its dynamics.

For Critchley, the ethical in deconstruction begins with the attempt to question the absorption by the ego, by the knowing self, of all that comes under its purview. This absorption is primarily identified with and warranted by philosophy as a set of cognitive theories that construe knowing as a subjection of differences to the same. In order to question this transmutation of the differing into, or its subjugation under, the same, the negation of alterity by intellectual advance must be recognized. This can only be done if one interrupts the advance by placing oneself not behind or within but outside or in front of knowing, in the particular that the process will absorb.

Critchley argues that deconstruction implies an ethic, and he combines Derrida and Levinas to formulate it. Derrida wants to create uncertainty and hesitation in the thinker; Levinas wants to locate the crucial moment outside of thinking, in attention to the face of the other person. In other words, both criticize the modern philosophical enterprise as granting a dominating power to acts of knowing. Knowing becomes a kind of machine that absorbs particularities into a huge sameness. The difference is that whereas Derrida tries to interrupt this process by wounding the thinker, the driver of the machine, Levinas interrupts it by taking a position outside of the machine and in the presence of what is about to be gobbled up. Critchley wants to combine these two ethical responses, arguing that the two clarify and reinforce one another.

Critchley elaborates the ethics of deconstructive practice by arguing that Derrida never was, and should not be taken as, located in what I have described as the first stage of postmodernism. Reading for Derrida has never been the kind of loose affair that is characteristic of that phase. For Derrida, a text is first read in a straightforward manner resulting in commentary, in an interpretation of what the text intends, and then it is read to destabilize that meaning by exposing not so much contradictions in the text's arguments as the exclusions and concealments that are included within the text's pretensions toward coherence and completeness. This second moment of reading wounds the thinker because the pretensions of adequacy driving the enterprise are exposed. Deconstruction thereby calls attention to what philosophy has not wanted to recognize and what it is unable to think. Deconstruction is an ethically motivated antiphilosophical/philosophical project; *"deconstruction is a 'philosophy' of hesitation . . . the* 'experience' of undecidability."[57]

For Levinas, the ethical is located outside of the thinking project and with the other, with the particular that will be absorbed by thinking. This relation to the face of the other is one of obligation and duty, and it is primary to the ethical. That primary relation cannot be forgotten or sublated by thinking, by attention to the inclusive or general.

For Critchley, then, postmodernist ethics is two-sided; it extricates the trace of "Saying" in the "Said" and tries to question or complicate the Said by locating Saying, the other, or alterity, as primary. Together they form an ethics that militates against modernist culture's "comprehensive claims to mastery."[58]

Critchley recognizes the distance between Derrida and Levinas. There is no way, for Derrida, to get out of the machine; all one can do is to cause hesitation in the driver, to question the enterprise and to expose its claims as spurious. Levinas takes a position outside or in front of the thinking process, in the presence or place of the one about to be absorbed. Although

Critchley relates the two as complementary, he also retains the gap between them, and it is there, in such an interstice, that he locates the ethical not as a position but as an uncertain location where one struggles to be faithful both to the general and to the particular. This means both belonging to a tradition, culture, or form of practice and being against them, neither completely identified with or completely free from them.[59] Such interstices can never become a position or a foundation. *"Ethics signifies enigmatically, as a determinate pattern of oscillation, or alteration. One might say that ethics signifies undecidably."*[60] Thought clarifies the ethical when it confronts, rather than eludes or conceals, its own contradictions.

However, Critchley wants to move out of dubiousness to action, for the political, which deconstruction largely lacks, cannot be avoided. One must make political decisions even though one makes them with uncertainty. For him, uncertainty makes political decisions ethical because, rather than dictated by theories of political immanentism and totality, political decisions made in the spirit of deconstruction posit the ethical as not articulated by the system, as outside the Said, and this keeps politics from being complete and finalized. The deconstructive contribution to politics is not so much in deploying new political models or strategies as in questioning the adequacy of the political, of pointing out always what is being excluded, repressed, or disfigured. Any attempt to bring certainty to politics must be countered by a move, in the direction of Derrida and Levinas, to subvert that certainty and to counter its violence. "Social space is an infinite splintering, or fragmentation, of space into spaces in which there is consequently a multiplication of political possibilities. Philosophy . . . is the discourse which, through its activity of open, agonistic critique, ensures that the community remains an open community, at the service of ethical difference."[61] The ethical is a counter-, critical, and/or corrective action.

There is much in this intricate contribution to a postmodernist ethics that deserves attention, and it represents, along with the other examples considered here, the rigor and intensity of this stage in postmodernist theory. But Critchley's ethics may be more convincing than the others primarily because it lacks content. It has a primarily negative function—to counter, prevent, or correct. As such it bears a striking resemblance to work of Richard Rorty and other American pragmatists. It is an ethic that looks like a strategy designed to serve the needs of an ongoing modernist project by correcting its excesses. By combining Levinas and Derrida, Critchley, rather than compound their force, modifies it in each and ends with neither a location nor a strategy of subversion.

I realize that to ask for content or norms in an ethics is to place the discourse within the system that it is the purpose of theory at this stage in postmodernism to destabilize and to question. Connor, by locating the ethical in particular kinds of discourses or texts, is unable to get outside the system or to articulate a norm by which these languages are both different from normal discourses and yet critical of and normative for them all. Wyschogrod, by positing a reality outside of textuality, sets limits on the extent to which discourse can affect both what we notice and why we might count it as exceptional. And Critchley, while he presents a position that stresses uncertainty, either throws us back into the first state of postmodernist theory and practice or gives us ways to modify or check the ongoing interests of the culture without bringing them radically into question. His ethic becomes a word of caution that only those already inclined to heed it will hear.

Perhaps these attempts at a postmodernist ethics disappoint because, to succeed, ethics seem to require a modernist scaffolding that can no longer be assumed or that has been torn away. What is needed first of all, then, is not an ethics but a cultural discipline from which ethics can again emerge.

All three of the stages in this part of the narrative, however, may contribute something to the next: the first contributes the retextualization of culture and reading as a definitive cultural practice; the second contributes the emphasis on functionally noncontingent values and on the world-enabling role of belief; and the third contributes three items, the importance of reading texts (Connor), the lure of exiting the culture (Wyschogrod), and the morality of uncertainty (Critchley).

CHAPTER FOUR

BLANCHOT AND KRISTEVA
Reading Scripture's Reappearance

In the final part of this narrative, reading a text as scripture, thoroughly dethroned by the surface orientation and instrumental or exchange notions of value and meaning that increasingly dominated modernity and set the terms for postmodernist culture, returns, like the ghost of Hamlet's father, an obscure figure, excluded but not forgotten, haunting the culture's margins. Its return, however faint, is nowhere more noticeable than in the work of Maurice Blanchot and Julia Kristeva. They oppose what reading in our culture has become and conduct us toward possibilities that can best be illuminated not by other postmodernist theories but by premodern understandings of reading such as implied by Calvin's doctrine of Scripture.

I turn first to the work of Blanchot and bring three matters to attention: why culture is rejected, how reading can be a way of rejecting the culture, and what results such reading can have for the culture. I then turn to Kristeva's theory of language acquisition and of reading as a process of total self-abjection. Since the orientation of Blanchot is more external and cultural and that of Kristeva more internal and psychological, they form, when placed together, a theory that resembles, in complexity, premodernist understandings of reading as epitomized in Calvin.

I

While Blanchot refers to our culture repeatedly, he does so in an unsystematic way and often indirectly. Consequently, his work does not offer a sustained and thorough cultural criticism or evidence to support the judgments he makes. This is because his analysis of culture is related to his theory of reading and is not freestanding. What can be done is to group his observations under a set of topics that relate the analysis of culture to the theory of reading.

One set of observations concerns our culture's addiction to answers. Blanchot thinks that answers have not only become more important than questions but also have created a culture that represses questions and dismisses those who question. A culture of answers is repressive and oppressive, and it severely limits the act of reading. For reading to be fully actualized, a condition of uncertainty must arise. For example, one can turn to those moments in the culture when people noticeably suffer injustice because of social, economic, and political forces. Such a move reveals that the answers of the culture or the culture of answers is never adequate, that there are always noticeable remainders of suffering that the answers ignore or discount. Consequently, one recognizes that "in the Yes of the answer we lose the direct, immediate given, and we lose the opening, the richness of possibility. The answer is the question's misfortune, its adversity."[1] Answers dominate and set the conditions of the culture because answers resemble commodities and appeal to the cultural desire to possess. Answers are abstracted from the questions that gave rise to them as commodities are abstracted from the conditions that produced them. Answers and commodities become possessions and are stored. Reading in a culture of accumulation is directed by and toward answers rather than questions. Indeed, when reading is placed in the service of questions it will appear to the culture of answers "to be dangerous, hostile and coldly violent."[2] In this culture reading is engaged as a practice that stabilizes answers. To oppose the culture, a very different kind of reading must be practiced.[3] This practice is not to be found among people who deliberately alienate themselves from the general culture, as have modernist readers and writers who, by means of arcane, elusive, or baffling texts, ascribe to themselves some privileged place. Reading against the culture is not a kind of transcendence or a claim for originality or moral superiority. Rather, reading against the culture arises from uncertainty and a willingness not to be taken seriously. It is, as with Kafka, not the assumption of a cognitive, aesthetic, or moral place above or apart from society but a willingness to have no place at all.

In addition to being distorted by the culture's addiction to answers and its repression of questions, reading is also distorted by the cultural desire for and imposition of unity. Whether this unity is one of system and sequence or one created by collagelike effects does not much matter; the culture wants unities and will produce them. There is an overriding obsession with the inclusive, the common denominator, and the socially encompassing. Blanchot suggests that the culture values unity and coherence in order to simplify and manipulate the world. The scientist is a cultural hero because the scientist has incorporated the cosmos into a putative unity by means of univocal language.[4] Blanchot sees this as a cultural characteristic built on the domination of Western thought by the idea of Logos, and he sees philosophy, even that of Heidegger, as unable to shake its addiction to the single, the central, the original, or the unified.[5] Consequently, it is difficult to separate language from the enterprises of unity, since our understanding of language serves our passion for incorporation. Even when one attends to something exceptional, something that lies outside the comprehension of language, such as disaster, language in such a culture as ours is always trying to integrate it into or subject it to some coherent or more significant whole.[6]

The knowledge to which our culture subjects reading is in itself or its consequences violent. This is noticeable in the metaphors of seeing and light that are often used to describe the act of gaining knowledge. One consequence of these metaphors is to think of knowing as an unmediated event, since light, which mediates the occasion of seeing, is easily overlooked.[7] The illusion of unmediated knowledge leads to violence. The notion that we can get at the truth, can get something or someone to yield up his or her secret, suggests torture and rape as analogous to the act of gaining knowledge.[8] Knowledge in our culture, consequently, is inseparable from violence.[9] True immediacy can never be assumed or forced.

Another metaphor that in our culture relates knowing to violence is grasping. Since our culture is one of accumulation and possession, the culturally prestigious act of learning, rather than stand apart, is subsumed by the ethos of grasping and hoarding and grants that ethos legitimacy. We operate with a unified notion of experience and knowledge, confronting every occasion or entity "as something we comprehend, grasp, bear, and master (even if we do so painfully and with difficulty) by relating it to Unity."[10] The metaphors of seeing and grasping that mark language about knowing reveal why centers of learning in the culture cannot object to cultural violence but must tacitly support it. Any tensions between centers of learning and the general culture are family squabbles or struggles for power.

Blanchot also detects violence in the current critique of intrinsic values. This does not mean that Blanchot wants to revive modernist theories of intrinsic value; indeed, the culture has relativized values, and this situation cannot be reversed. But he does want to emphasize that the loss of intrinsic values means that the violence perpetrated by knowing can now go on unimpeded. "This new authorization given to man when the authority of values has collapsed means first of all: knowing everything is permitted, there is no longer a limit to man's activity."[11] Not only that, science and the knowledge industry take to themselves the intrinsic value that once was thought to reside in various entities and events.

Blanchot's analysis of the nature and function of knowing in our culture complicates his politics. The general control of political theory and analysis by rational principles has distorted our understanding of political life. Rationality in political and social thought sublimates particular people to a common analysis or political solution. Blanchot relates this assessment of the political in our world to his position as a Jew. The holocaust is no exception to the interests and directions of modern politics but is symptomatic of them. Blanchot writes with the holocaust always as his political background, so that he posits reading not as continuous with the political tendencies of the culture but as a radical exception to them. The politics of his theory of reading are directed toward the possibility of another arrangement or another set of tendencies altogether. It takes its position with the marginalized and oppressed not to move them toward inclusion within the culture of answer, unity, and violence but to take their position as a site that leads toward an exit, a point, that is, if one may speak that way, not of "final solution," a phrase typical of the culture, but of final question.[12] Blanchot's is a postcultural politics, a politics not complicitous with the culture of oppression and violence, and its passivity is far from innocuous and innocent.

Blanchot, by using the spatial language of exit, also implies a critique of the culture's temporality, oriented as it is to the future. That future is determined and defined by what the culture projects, which are only possibilities that confirm and are continuous with itself. Readers directed toward an exit from the culture are oriented to and by possibilities neither incorporated in nor projected by the culture.[13] Consequently, when he proposes his theory of reading, he does so in terms that the culture would designate not only as impertinent but also as impossible. That which eludes or escapes the culture's understanding of the pertinent and possible no longer participates in the future, therefore, and finds its location spatially—that is, on the outside.

Finally, Blanchot judges that the culture, by subjecting language to use or instrumental value, removes the possibility of reading. Language must be freed from this subjection if reading is again to emerge. Language has been subjected to our "concern for results, the desire to have, the greed that links us to possession, the need for security, the tendency to know in order to be sure, the tendency to 'take account' which necessarily becomes an inclination to count and to reduce everything to accounts—the very destiny of the modern world."[14] One way of resisting this subjection of language to use is by attending to pointless language, and Blanchot thinks of poetic and fictive uses of language as to some degree marking sites where it may be possible to find idle language and, by means of it, an exit from the determinations of the culture. However, culture is indefatigable in its capacity to take what at first seems dissonant into its unity; today's anticultural departure is tomorrow's coveted wall hanging. "Literature" becomes the category that takes possession of idle or dissonant writing and reading, and the aesthetic incorporates as a cultural service.[15] It is for this reason that a theory of reading as exit will not arise in literary circles.

Our culture, given these general characteristics—the addiction to answers and unity because of the stabilization they provide, the violent nature of knowing recognizable in the reigning metaphors of seeing and grasping, the move that knowledge industries make from the demise of intrinsic value to ascribing intrinsic value to themselves, the domination of politics by rationality and the loss of particularity, the confinement of humanity within culturally dictated notions of the future, and the subjection of language to instrumental and exchange values—cannot offer terms for a theory of reading as a form of exit. Culturally determined notions of language, literature, and, above all, reading are to be discarded.

Another way to put all of this is to say that in the culture books are read. The culture fetishizes the result, the Book, the achievement of reading, rather than addressing the process, because it values the dead rather than the living, the commodity rather than the work. As Blanchot says, "[T]he book is to writing what death would be to the movement of dying; one can say that writing, dying are what are most discreet, although always made known by the public Last Act, the great tomb-like rock of the Book, the sovereign publication of absent presence."[16] The Book conceals the work, makes it invisible.[17] For Blanchot, reading as exit resists the Book and reads toward its absence. Reading moves toward the uncertainty or suffering that the Book covers and conceals.

It is clear that Blanchot's theory of reading will have nothing in common with reader-response theory, which is symptomatic of the culture and fully expresses the culture's understanding of reading as acquisition and self-extension. Blanchot's theory of reading stands in contrast to reading as carried on and explicated by the culture. But it must also be added that he does not set out as his alternative notions of intrinsic value that have been discredited. He will argue not for the value of the text but for the process of reading as a way not of gaining value but of losing it, not of appropriating but of divesting.

Blanchot's theory of reading will also free readers from the authority of critics. Critics tell readers what to read and how to read the texts they deem important. "The critic," he says, "is there to come between book and reader. He represents the decisions and the paths of culture. . . . He says what we must read and how we must read it, finally rendering reading useless. . . . Hence the result that if there has never been written as much as there is today, we are nonetheless gravely and painfully deprived of reading."[18] This would not be quite so bad if critics were good readers, but they read with only an eye to what there might be in the reading that they could use as a basis for their own advancement. While our culture is enamored with the possibility of unmediated knowledge, when it comes to reading we look for the mediation of critics, for priestly authority. But reading as exit is a process on which one embarks alone. It is only in uncertainty that one may be able to engage reading as an exit from the culture.[19] Blanchot is willing to call uncertainty "fear," "*the fear that is produced by nothing in particular, except nights without sleep, days without wakefulness, desire for that which provokes the fear that nothing provokes.*"[20]

Blanchot's theory also will not construe reading as a pastime or a profession; reading is not reserved as an occasional or a specialized act. Indeed, we read all the time, and reading is characteristic of the human condition.[21] Blanchot can be taken as wanting to substitute for the culturally formative and prestigious claim "I think" the uncertain and process-suggestive alternative, "I read."

While Blanchot projects reading as discontinuous with culture, he assumes an at least partial distinction between culture and language. This becomes clear when he posits language as the site where or the occasion when reading against the culture can begin. One kind of language that may be countercultural is interrogation. Any question can lead to an interrogation of the whole, and this potential in any question gives it the hint or prospect of ultimacy. The question of the whole is the question to which all questions point, and it is for this reason that questions are resisted in the culture.[22] They are resisted because, like pebbles that start avalanches, they may lead to destabilizing the whole.[23] Because the culture resists questions and does not provide a language by which it, as a whole, can be interrogated, the culture, rather than questioned, must be fled.[24] Reading provides an occasion for that act.[25] Questions lead toward exit the more they have within and behind them the resonance of disaster, of the unspeakable.[26] The language of the culture contains within it what normally it is employed to resist or conceal, namely, such revealing or culture-defining disasters as the holocaust.[27]

Language not only occasions interrogations of the culture and reveals traces of the culture's violence, it also hints at things left out by the culture. Words can awaken things forgotten, excluded, or repressed by the culture, and when such speak, they carry a peculiar, even sacred, force. They provide a language that seems to contain revelations.[28] When language of the excluded or excluded language comes into writing, it brings sacrality to writing, and when excluded language is read, it has the force of the outside and changes everything, no matter how slightly.

Language also has potential to suggest the writer's or reader's particularity. Language may at some moments bring something specific and peculiar to attention, an alternative to the generalizing, totality-serving directions of the culture. When this occurs, the possibility of the postlapsarian question about location put by God to Adam is faintly repeated: "Where are you?"[29] That kind of question, when raised by language's faint exposure of particular locations, displaces the writer or reader from his or her position as defined by the whole. Then the reader attends to the writer differently, not simply as a writer but as a specific other. This shift is as close as we can come in our culture, for Blanchot, to what it might mean to hear God speaking in human language. For, as Jacob says to Esau, God is to be seen in the face of human presence. Although language can convey singularity, it normally does not in our culture because the singular is passed over as a not yet integrated quirk.[30]

This is not to say that Blanchot revives a category of religious language; he considers religious language to be subsumed under cultural determinations. Rather, Blanchot has Freud in mind. Freud exposed the capacity of language not only to bring to the surface matters hidden by and to the analysand but also to bring the analysand out of one world and into an at least partially altered one.[31] Biblical quotations, which are numerous in Blanchot's work, stand more as examples of a potential in language than as having in themselves particular religious properties, and he sees those potentials in poetic language of our own day as well. However, the name of God has force in our culture by virtue of the death of God, by the name's emptiness and pointlessness. If the word, now fallen from significant cultural use, has force, it does so as a kind of cultural Freudian slip.[32]

Finally, literary language, while it also has been incorporated by the strategies of self-legitimation in the culture, indicates a moment or a place where uncertainties, at least momentarily, can appear. This is because there is often a delay between the uncertainty created by literary language and the incorporation of that language by cultural institutions. The literary in our culture is itself always a question, and however momentarily or partially, it stands apart from the culture.[33] Literary departures are temporary, but they do suggest the singular. Literary language retains a potential for exit so long as it has not yet been assigned a cultural place and role.[34]

Blanchot's theory of reading, then, arises from his description of the prevailing culture, particularly what this culture does to language, his partial distinction of language from culture, and his belief that language provides occasions or sites that indicate exit from the culture. Exits are not, however, readily available; they are recognized only with concentrated effort or by chance. And they must be approached in ways that will not subsume them to a culture eager to overcome dissonance and difference by reduction to and inclusion within the whole. Exit is not incorporated by language; there is no language of exit. Exit is actualized in and by particular practices of reading.

II

One characteristic of Blanchot's theory of reading is that he does not distinguish clearly between reading and writing and does not elevate one or the other. This means that what he says about writing can be translated into reading and vice versa. His intention is not to raise the prestige of the reader to that of the writer, as occurs in so much current literary theory, but rather to place on the reader uncertainties and burdens equal to those that are the lot of the writer. The kind of reading that Blanchot has in mind, the kind that leads to exit from the culture, places reading in a key altogether different from what we are accustomed.

One ingredient in Blanchot's theory of reading is particularization. Although deluded by ideologies of individuality, people in our culture are anything but particularized, and Blanchot is not advocating the kind of individuality that this culture leads us to think we already have. Nor is particularity personal, a cultivation of personal idiosyncrasy. Indeed, personality and individuality are both products of the culture. Particularizing the reader, in fact, means rejecting individuality and personality. One could more accurately call it anonymity, the loss of individuality and personality in the quotidian. "In the everyday we have no name, little personal reality, scarcely a figure, just as we have no social determination to sustain or enclose us."[35] The quotidian that fosters anonymity is found anywhere and nowhere, especially in the streets of cities. The quotidian resists all in the culture that pretends to grant distinction. To be absorbed by the everyday is to enter the nihilism at the heart of culture that the culture conceals. To treat anonymity as that to which the culture leads is to begin exiting the culture by way of what the culture most fully is. The anonymity the culture produces has the usual effect of compelling people to actions and postures of gaining attention, of standing out from the crowd. To accept the anonymity of the everyday is to reduce the chances of the violence implicit in attention-getting acts. Anonymity is the mode of behavior suited to a situation of violence. In a concentration camp the last thing one wants is to be noticed, is to have one's name recognized or called.[36]

Another way Blanchot indicates this loss of significance is by means of the neuter. While the negative participates dialectically in the culture, the neuter has no cultural role or significance. It suggests simple thereness. When entered and attended to, simple thereness begins to emerge as a contrary to the culture, not as a negative but as something meaningless that the culture creates but has no place for. Because it has no place, the neuter cannot be integrated.[37] The location of the everyday and the neuter are points where language unravels, where, dissociated from cultural determinations, it comes apart or becomes strange.[38] The strangeness that language assumes when no use or institution claims or stands behind it makes language unpredictable, like utterances of oracles that have no identifiable source and no particular meaning.[39] The reader, entering language so located, does not enter a more revealing language, however. It is a language that belongs to no one, that no one speaks, that is addressed to no one, that has no center, and that reveals nothing.[40] To enter the anonymous and the neuter is not at all like arriving someplace, of locating or being located somewhere, but entering it is indispensable to particularization.

Bereft of the confirmations that cultural locations and the illusion of individuality give, a person loses confidence and certainty, and fear, fright, and disorientation take their place. We "experience in the guise of the frightening what is entirely outside us and other than us: the outside itself."[41] In a culture of confidence, reassurances, answers, and certainty, uncertainty, dubiousness, and fear mark the exit.

Finally, particularization requires renunciation and solitude. One way in which Blanchot talks of this condition is in reference to being Jewish in a dominantly non-Jewish world. To be Jewish is to be destined to dispersion, called "to a sojourn without place." Being Jewish removes the possibility and forbids the temptation of "Unity-Identity."[42] To be Jewish is to have a "relation to exteriority."[43] Particularization, because it requires renunciation and solitude, does not mean having a stable self or unified ego; "I" is a category only theology can sustain. An "I" is not an atheist, for the language of God has always privileged the single, unified, and initiatory that the "I" wants above all in this culture to protect.[44] *Dépaysement*, being out of one's element and proper place, is crucial to the reading that leads to exit.[45] "I read" becomes for Blanchot an actual or potential oxymoron.

Solitude is not self-containment or self-sufficiency, therefore. Solitude is noninteriority, and it can only be found on the outside. The solitary person is one deprived of meaning and location.[46] Such a person becomes in the culture an object of suspicion, a puzzle to others and to self.[47] Like the characters of Kafka's novels, the position of such a person is awkward. The solitary person is exposed to the ambiguities of existence as the coherences and supports of the culture are stripped away.[48] The reader becomes an exile, and the exile "remains separated, where the deep of dissimulation reigns, that elemental obscurity through which no way can be made and which because of that makes its awful way through him."[49] What usually passes for solitude is self-absorption and autonomy, a subjectivity declaring its independence from, even its mastery over, other entities. But solitude for Blanchot is a condition in which the "I" dissolves, in which nothing substantial or unified remains.

Given the strenuous and exacting conditions of exit from the culture, it is not at all clear in Blanchot that a person, especially given the kinds of reassurances and certainties that the culture provides, would be willing to undertake reading as exit and exile. It is not that when one flees, one enters another, truer world or comes to a truer sense of self. What one comes to is a disorienting desert and a dissolving of the putative unity of the self. Why would the reader follow the occasions that language provides for moving toward such exit and loss?

One answer to this question is the sense of lack that the culture creates. Something is missing, concealed, or denied, and the lack indicates that something is terribly wrong. Being a Jew makes one more sensitive than otherwise to the possibilities of such telltale lacks.[50] Awareness of lack does not arise from antisocial trespasses, for to transgress is only to come up against some further cultural boundary that must then also be transgressed. Transgression implicates a person more fully within the confines of the culture. Nor is lack something that will complete or enhance the person. Rather, lack indicates "the other as other, a desire that is austere, disinterested, without satisfaction, without nostalgia, unreturned, and without return."[51] At the center of his theory of reading Blanchot posits lack as an irresistible lure, not the Siren's song (although he uses that trope), because the Siren's song is something, while lack and its appeal are nothing, but the lure of disorientation, of deprivation, of radical interrogation, of unrelieved uncertainty. Lack lures by avoiding articulation. Lack has no actual or potential content. It is difficult to account for the attraction of lack, to give an explanation of it. As Foucault says, "Attraction is no doubt for Blanchot what desire is for Sade, force for Nietzsche, the materiality of thought for Artaud, and transgression for Bataille: the pure, most naked, experience of the outside."[52]

Reading is a response to the lure of the lack and the exit to which it leads. It is a response to an obscure and indefinite (im)possibility. "We believe that we think the strange and the foreign, but in reality we never think anything but the familiar; we think not the distant, but the close that measures it."[53] The exit becomes a contentless, nondirected response to the question implied by lack, and reading is the way in which that exit is approached.[54]

The process of reading that leads from lack to exit involves forgetting. One must bring to reading, as to writing, not the habits and skills acquired for gaining knowledge but the willingness to forget them. Forgetting is for Blanchot an important but neglected aspect of philosophy, for it is only by forgetting that we can know something other than what we knew before. We need to exclude in order for something that is not the same to occur to us. Another way of saying this is that reading is a process of learning what it might mean in this instance to read in opposition to previous acts of reading, against the habits of confirming or extending the self and culture. Such reading Blanchot refers to as the search for the work in the Book. It is a reading not so much of the words as of the question or suffering within them. Like calling forth Lazarus from the tomb, reading a text can make contact with the dying that has become entombed within the Book. Since the Book is culture's repression of the questions, lacks, and sufferings that gave rise to it, reading must be a reading toward "*the absence of the book.*"[55] Read not in the direction of the Book but against it, toward uncertainty, suffering, and loss.[56]

Such reading is marked not by goal and accomplishment but by fascination and purposelessness. Fascination is contrary to seeing, for in fascination there is openness to imprinting, a passivity to the power of what one encounters. Fascination changes the reader's relation to language.[57] Fascination and purposelessness take one outside of time, outside the determinations of a task and a goal, and one has an altogether different relation to language.[58] Goal and accomplishment favor the Book and repress the work; they put suffering out of reach by not allowing reading to suffer.[59]

A good time for such reading is late at night, night without sleep, night that has no relation to the day. Blanchot has much to say about the night. Solitude and exile are suited to the night. The familiar connections and reassurances of the daylight world, its habits and stabilities, are left behind by night. The goals of the day dwindle in importance, and uncertainty with loss of purpose arises. Sleep, he says, belongs to the day, in that it is daytime's use of the night. Sleep blots out the night.[60] Sleep is the affirmation that, despite differences and tensions that may exist between me and my culture, we are basically on the best of terms. Insomnia, however, exposes night in all its alien and forceful character. Without sleep safely to transport us from one day to the next, we are abandoned to the night, and the night of sleeplessness becomes distant from and hostile to the day. Once given over to the night, we are unable to sleep. Fatigue sets in, then anxiety, and finally a sickening of self and of the daylight world. Such nights are the sites of solitude, and reading in such a state will not be an escape from the night nor an extension of service to the day but will intensify the loss of day. Under such conditions one is frightfully uncertain whether the world will ever again be restored, whether one is permanently condemned to the darkness and disorientation of night.

Night as disconnected from day is a faint simulacrum of disaster, particularly the disaster of the holocaust. This is a place unrelated to normality, yet it is a place produced by the normal. In it no affirmations can be made, no assurance given, no direction charted. Moments of disorientation, along with all instances of oppression, injustice, deprivation, and anxiety, are echoes or faint indications of disasters such as the holocaust. All such moments suggest a nullity into which one is likely to sink and which one is not able to articulate, indeed, where language becomes useless.[61] Night, oppression, injustice, and disaster counter language. It is not even possible to question them. Indeed, one cannot even speak of experiencing them. It is only later, in retrospect, that they can be addressed. Such moments suggest the total absence of meaning, the place where nothing could be questioned, let alone affirmed, and they lie beneath the surface of the culture in the holocaust. A culture that wants above all to deny disaster compels the reader toward exit.

Exit from the culture, while effected by acts of reading, is finally a form of passivity. Blanchot compares it to the divestment and passivity of dying: "*Dying-dying in the cold and dissolution of the Outside: always outside oneself as outside life.*"[62] The passivity he has in mind is unlike what generally that word connotes: "It is very difficult for us—and thus all the more important—to speak of passivity, for it does not belong to the world, and we know nothing which would be utterly passive (if we did, we would inevitably transform it)."[63] Indeed, passivity is never passive enough. Reading is like dying, no longer to have power, unity, or direction.[64] It is not so much a passive way of reading as it is "passivity's reading," a "nocturnal vigil."[65] It is only in this way that the work can be read, that there can be a rapprochement between the reader and the work concealed by the Book.[66] And the reader who dies there does not soon revive or use the dying to secure something new. Nothing comes of dying.

One of the characteristics of reading toward the outside Blanchot refers to as plural reading. He distrusts monologues or long, unbroken discourses. He emphasizes pauses, breaks, and differences, and he advocates fragmentary writing and reading. Fragments are more important than what relates them to one another; they indicate the unspoken and, perhaps, the unspeakable. Fragmented reading and writing resist the cultural norms of purpose, goal, and unity.[67] The pauses of fragmented writing do not indicate deeper meanings; they indicate the uncertainty that lies within all of speech. When one reads and writes in fragments, the contraries of "surface and depth, real and possible, above and below, manifest and hidden" are routed.[68]

Blanchot describes reading as indirect. Like Orpheus, one cannot look exit in the face. One needs to back up to it while also not falling into it. Here, perhaps, it is appropriate to use the phrase "as though," which has appeared at various points throughout this work. The "as though" is not hypothetical, a pretense or an illusion; nor is it a construction of the reader. Reading, like dying, is not a project and makes no claims. One reads "as though . . ."

The final thing that I want to say about Blanchot's theory of reading is that he punctuates and illustrates it with many references to biblical narratives. I mention this not to sanctify it but to offer another answer to the question why one would read toward the exits from culture. Although Blanchot implies several answers to this question—sensitivity to lack, to the sufferings of forgotten and oppressed people, and to the violence of a culture that needs to be abjured—to the question, that is, why, given the hardships, divestment, and fright involved, one would turn to the outside rather than cling to the securities, however fallacious, of the culture, the most intriguing answer arises from the biblical subtext in his work. He cites biblical narratives as directives for this kind of reading; biblical patterns suggest what it might mean to read. The stories of the patriarchs, of Abraham leaving his home to journey to a foreign and difficult place or called on to sacrifice his son, his future, of Jacob wrestling with the night messenger at the crossing of the Jabbok brook, of the exodus from Egypt, the wandering in the wilderness, the exile into Babylon and the diaspora—all these references and more are used by Blanchot to illustrate what he means by reading. This use has two consequences. First, it indicates that he takes the narratives of the Bible as implicit theories concerning how to read—minimally, as how the Bible wants to be read as a work rather than as a Book. Second, it indicates that Blanchot recognizes in the Bible patterns that convey to readers who have ears to hear what it might mean to learn again how to read. This in no way is intended to imply that Blanchot brings in, by way of these references, a theology of some kind. What I mean is that, for Blanchot, biblical texts suggest the de-familiarizing that constitutes the principal consequence of reading the texts as scripture.

III

The final point around which one can construct a theory of reading from Blanchot's fragments is, of the three, the least developed. This is due not to a lack of rigor or attention but to the very nature of its particular focus. The third matter is the consequence of reading, and this cannot be developed because the results must remain uncertain. Were one to have the results of reading clearly set out, they would become the goal of reading; and if there were a goal of reading, it would not be reading of the sort that Blanchot projects. Yet Blanchot recognizes the awkward matter that the reader does not remain at the exit; life goes on, daylight returns, and the culture must be in some way reentered and reengaged. What can be said, then, about the reader who has entered the space of the work and has had at least some exposure to the exit and now must, in a centrifugal direction, return to the culture?

The first thing to say is that in some respects nothing is changed; nothing is gained, nothing can be taken from the event of reading, no information, no message, no truth. In reading, language has been dissociated from world, author, and reference and has become "only a scandalous semblance of truth, an image, and by its imagery and seeming draws away truth into depths where there is neither truth nor meaning, not even error."[69] The consequence of reading does not even have, then, the force or significance of negativity: "Rather than a purely negative mode, it is, on the contrary, a time without negation, without decision, when here is nowhere as well, and each thing withdraws into its image while the 'I' that we are recognizes itself by sinking into the neutrality of a featureless third person."[70] To read is to find the point where here and nowhere merge, where language is all there is, language with nothing behind it, a presence that is indistinguishable from absence, language as an image of itself. This means that the uncertainty that marks reading is not replaced, when reading ends, by some other, let us say, transcendental certainty. Rather, if the reading is carried to the point Blanchot indicates, it renders the reader radically uncertain. When we speak of the results of reading according to Blanchot, then, we have to use "results" in a peculiar way. They have the status more of luck, chance, or the unexpected than of gain, and they have nothing to do with possession. Reading produces nothing.

One "result" may be familiarity with absence. Absence interrogates without itself being interrogated.[71] It comes to the reader in the form of language when language has ceased to be a way of knowing or of having a world.[72] The reading that Blanchot projects is, in other words, a process by which the reader's relation to the Other is altered. Ordinarily, the Other is what I cannot grasp, because it transcends me and serves as a beyond for which I long as completion. But in reading, the Other, rather than the distant to which I am related, comes to me as an absence that is all too near and that opens distance, "dis-identifying me, abandoning me to passivity, leaving me without any initiative and bereft of present."[73]

Other as absence can also become the face of another person, one that is unknown to me or has suddenly become enigmatic.[74] This point makes Blanchot look like Levinas, but Blanchot does not *begin* with a relation to the other as a basis, however elusive and unstable, for ethics; rather, the other *comes* to me, and relation to the other cannot be explicated in moral or in any other terms. The other who comes to me as another person does so without any common ground between us; there is no relationship posited by a common humanity, by suffering, or even by a common language. Finally, the other that comes to me in human form is not a personality, is not a self, is not substantial. It is, rather, the human as it emerges in and from the work, from the writing or reading, and from the suffering. This is not the cultural corpse of the author or the cultural agent of the conversational partner; the other comes to me, however faintly, from the outside. The other comes to me more like those who appear, unexpectedly and often disconcertingly, in dreams[75] or, perhaps even better, who appear, as does the ghost of Hamlet's father, as one identified with night and with death, as one who brings the whole situation, including myself, into question.[76] At the exit, the cultural distinctions between real and unreal, possible and impossible, and normal and abnormal are blurred, and the recognition of the other in the one who comes to me cannot be analyzed and evaluated in terms set by the culture to which that coming and that outside have no direct relation, have only the standing of lack.

A third "result" of reading is that exits mark places. They are analogous to places where people have died, places that previously had been ordinary but now are anything but ordinary. One thinks, for example, of how often flowers are left at some place on a street where a person important to some others has, by accident or another's hand, been killed. Such spots are not cultural monuments; they are arbitrary places imprinted on the minds of people because someone important to them died there. In addition, exits are like the faces of people who have died. The face of the dead, because it does not look back at us and because death makes an image of the person, is more like the person than the person's living face.[77] Similarly, the exit exposed by reading is marked, and the reader takes on an image formed by it. Particularly, this consequence applies to language as now marked by exits, because language, when released from use and cultural determinations, becomes an image of itself, becomes more like itself than when engaged.[78]

These "results" are not contributions to the culture and are of no direct use in it; rather, an alteration occurs for the reader regarding what reading is, what may appear in other faces, and how language is constituted. Blanchot suggests that the return is as from a biblical desert, "where the covenant originates."[79] In the desert there is immediacy that makes the culture, once near and familiar, now strange. While what comes to the reader has no content or application, it alters the reader by rendering all in the culture as distant, endlessly mediated, and radically questionable.

In addition, the metaphor of covenant is appropriate for the kind of future thrust that Blanchot gives to the "results" of reading. Language as other, or the language of the other, has not only a dislocating consequence for the reader who returns to the culture, it also has a future possibility (or impossibility). It can be used to indicate a future unrelated to the controlled future of the culture. Because this language does not speak and bears no message, it has potential as a language of a discontinuous future, "always ahead of itself, with its meaning and its legitimacy always ahead of it."[80] Because this future separates me from a future that is my own or that the culture has in mind for me, it is dislocating, and Blanchot does not hesitate to refer to the language and behavior of Old Testament prophets and to oracles not for their predictive roles but for the violence by which they and their hearers are wrenched from their expected futures and held in suspension for a future unrelated to anything else.

Blanchot goes further. He believes it is possible for the reader to begin to gather in things from the culture, not to possess or use them but to shelter them, as Noah took the animals into the ark for protection. One can retrieve things from the culture's placements or uses and relate them to a different time and space.[81] In that space and time things can be transformed. Because they are not possessed or used, they occasion dispossession and provoke uncertainty.[82] Such things constitute a noncultural space that is pointless and invisible, a waiting place. Indeed, such a space is not a space as such, and things in it are not things any longer.[83] Unintegrated, they adumbrate a future where unexpected possibilities might occur.

The reader cannot identify with or dwell in exits but must return to the culture. However, the reader is now divided. The reader comes back to the culture with some sense that there may be other possible worlds or ways by which things can be "worlded." Having been detached from this culture, the reader is susceptible to the other worlds that language may portend. Such possibilities remain impossible to the culture, however, for otherwise the culture would appropriate them, if nothing else, as literature.[84]

The reader carries on in the culture, then, as a divided person. The reader behaves strangely, at times unpredictably and senselessly. The reader is in no position to relate the culture reentered to an exit because the culture and the exit cannot take one another into account; they are alien to one another. The reader is no mediator, no messenger, no composite and can work or look for no *Aufhebung* of the difference. While, as I said, small changes can be made—things gathered, language newly regarded, people treated as other, fascination replacing impatience—it is unlikely that these actions or attitudes will change anything at all, and no appreciation of them can be expected from the culture. Nonetheless, the culture no longer has a hold on or sway over the reader, who now knows what it is like, or at least might be like, to be somewhere else.

IV

Although the contrast should not be made too sharply, it can be said that Judaism and Christianity differ, among other ways, in that delivery in Judaism is from one's enemies and delivery in Christianity is from one's self. Although both contain both, the differing emphases recur. And they do in the work of Blanchot in contrast to that of Julia Kristeva. While, again, both contain both, the stress of Blanchot is delivery from the culture, from its deceptions and violence. Kristeva stresses reading not so much as release and separation from the culture as divestment or abjection of something internal to the reader. The contrary emphases or directions of Blanchot and Kristeva, along with the many interests that they have in common, allow them to be treated as complementary to one another.

Kristeva, in constructing reading as a process of self-divestment, locates the moment of acquiring language with separation and rejection. The child exchanges the immediacy of wants and needs supplied by the mother for language as a general system of indicators of those needs; language use displaces prior immediacy. Language, then, is always associated with loss and lack. This means that language is always implicated in the dynamics of desire for that which is lost, and language is always threatened by that desire.

Language and the self that uses language become protections from and concealments of loss and lack. A defiant and insistent self-enclosedness results. In order to avoid such narcissism, abjection of the self and its language must occur. The self must be not the sponsor or beneficiary of language but its abject. This means that "I spit *myself* out, I abject *myself* with the same motion through which 'I' claim [linguistically] to establish *myself*."[85] Abjection of the self implies the recognition that the "I" and its language are based on nothing, are suspended over an inaugural loss: "There is nothing like the abjection of self to show that all abjection is in fact recognition of the *want* on which any being, meaning, language, or desire is founded." Abjection is not only negative, however; it is a move against the self in the name or memory of that moment from which the self arises, of that from which language and identity separate one. "Abjection is a resurrection that has gone through death (of the ego). It is an alchemy that transforms the death drive into a start of life, of new significance." But that process is not easily undertaken, because identity and language become protections from abjection. Kristeva recognizes ambivalence toward abjection in the rituals of traditional societies, in psychoanalysis, and in reading, particularly reading poetry. She analyzes all of these processes in terms of the complex relation between language, with the order and identity it grants, and what language must reject before it can confer these benefits and the repression that these benefits imply. The abject, then, cannot remain external to a person: "'There is an abject' is henceforth stated as, 'I am abject, that is, mortal and speaking.' "[86]

Abjection of self is, according to Kristeva, fully assumed by or described in the New Testament, especially in Saint Paul, and in such Christian writers as Saint Augustine, Saint Bernard of Clairvaux, and Saint Thomas Aquinas. The principal threat to a person's well-being comes not from the outside but from within, and a purgation, a divestment of the self, becomes fully integrated into spiritual disciplines. Sin, and its close relations to death, and a sense of the definitive relation of sin and death to the self become for Christianity what the "enemy" is for Judaism: "[S]in is set forth as constitutive of man, coming to him from the depth of his heart, thus recalling the original sin of Adam."[87] The abject is not that which one is furthest from but the point, despite its contradiction, closest to purity. It is the point where the flesh in its defilement clarifies the spirit.

Narcissism counters abjection because narcissism is a condition of containment within the self's language and an unawareness of that containment. It is the position of a person who takes representations as though they were actual and who operates in a self-reflective and static world. The principal consequence of this condition lies in human relationships; the narcissist cannot love.[88] A condition prevalent in, if not characteristic of, the culture, narcissism is a radically unethical state.[89] Subversion or abjection of this condition arises not from moral norms but from practices by which identities and locations are destabilized.

Kristeva identifies reading as a crucial practice for destabilization. Reading suggests the psychoanalytic situation, one also important for Blanchot, as a principal site for exchanging narcissism and related impasses for the process of reconstituting a speaking subject related to others.[90] Processes of reconstituting cannot occur without faith, trust, and transferential love. In the context they provide, the analysand/reader at least partially sheds a former self and recognizes, again perhaps only partially, a new self.[91] The reader finds in the text not simply the surface but, more important, the genotext, the tortured and heterogeneous languages constitutive of it, what Blanchot calls the "work." Reading the genotext results not in appropriation or use of the text but in speaking with it or being spoken to.[92]

Kristeva posits love and forgiveness as crucial to transformations of the self that release it from narcissism and that reconstitute relations. Love and forgiveness form a kind of third party, a context or space for reading in which tranferences and transformations can occur. Narcissists construe the third party as a negative, prohibitive factor—the laws, for example, that young lovers may be flouting by their embrace—a factor that creates or intensifies relations by the negative means of prohibition and imagined threat. But when love is the third party, displacing the negative stimulant of prohibition with unconditional regard, it creates and intensifies not desire so much as *jouissance*, a transformation of body, desire, and self. This *jouissance* is a moment, in a higher form, of reconciliation with that from which, by acquiring language, a person was once separated as the rejecting and rejected. Kristeva explicates this role of love and forgiveness in relation to premodern, especially Christian, materials and locates its contemporary possibilities primarily in psychoanalysis and in reading poetry: "[T]he literary experience stands revealed as an essentially amorous experience, unstabilizing the same through its identification with the other." "The space of love is the space of writing [and reading]."[93]

Kristeva deploys this triadic model of speakers and the surrogate body of love and forgiveness in contrast to options provided both by deconstruction and by political analyses. Deconstruction provides a kind of reading determined by narcissistic tendencies, a reading wholly defined by signifiers in which no *other* can be taken seriously. Moreover, the radical relativizing that deconstruction produces renders impossible the experience of what is and is not true or right for an analytical session: "The analyst, who is under the ethical obligation to try to cure her patients, is not free to say whatever she likes, to engage in the free play of the signifiers. Instead, there *is* a truth in analysis: a correct intervention or a mistaken one."[94] On the other side she contrasts the surrogate body of love and forgiveness to political, especially Marxist, reading because the latter has no place either for the subject or for meaning.[95] Political analysis emphasizes what is shared and external, whereas the reading that Kristeva theorizes emphasizes differences and the irreducibility of the individual to the whole.[96] She makes note of these contrasts not to dismiss deconstructive or political reading but to counter their putative adequacy and to advocate an alternative to them, a theory that posits the possibility of reading as an occasion or process of self-abjection and reconstitution.

Reading holds this potential because there are possibilities of language not co-opted by the socially stabilizing functions of communication. Desire and suffering displace social stabilization. Reading also can attend to multiplicity implicit in language—Kristeva has a strong interest in Dostoyevsky and Bakhtin. And she positions the reader as one who "would search within the signifying phenomenon for the *crisis* of the *unsettling process* of meaning and subject rather than for the coherence or identity of either *one* or a *multiplicity* of structures."[97] Reading so engaged follows a path of suffering and rejection that leads to an acceptance of death, which is itself a kind of death. As in Holbein's depiction of the dead Christ in his tomb, this death carries "not the slightest suggestion of transcendency," although embracing death and allowing desire to die have a certain consequence because their power over the person ends.[98] The reader can follow this path and enter this space because the text forgives, and forgiveness creates the context where abjection, the loss of desire and the recognition of death, not only can be carried on to finality but inhabited and traversed.[99]

The theories of Blanchot and Kristeva, yoked together, yield a way of reading that does not privilege either the external or the internal, the cultural or the personal—a theory of the practice of reading that counters both the culture and the self and that leads to the possibility of reentering culture and reemerging as a speaking self. Together they provide an account of reading identifiable as a site of reading scripture's faint return.

CONCLUSION
Reading the Bible As Though It Were Scripture

In the Introduction I proposed that a theory of textuality requires the category of scripture. Such a category illumines the role of texts in locating a person or group on the textual field, and it suggests both how it is that persons and groups have worlds and how it occurs that their worlds are confirmed and challenged. I then went on briefly to describe biblical texts in such a way as to account, at least partially, for the fact that the Bible for so many people and for so long has functioned as scripture. I pointed out, for example, that the Bible, while culturally specific, is also highly transportable, so that people in diverse situations and over centuries have located themselves in relation to biblical texts. And I pointed out that biblical texts, not only because of their cultural diversity but also because of their differing responses to uncertainties arising from all four of the ingredients required for the formation of a world, could effectively perform the functions both of granting a world and of challenging it. That is, I suggested that there could be more than accidental relations between the textual category of scripture and biblical texts. I conclude now with a third suggestion of this kind: the Bible serves well as scripture because it instructs the reader how it should be read, how to read it as scripture.

This comment on the principal direction of biblical texts has been prepared by reading Blanchot and Kristeva. Although different from one another in many ways, they can be seen as clarifying a cultural practice that may once again become possible, namely, reading texts as scripture. Their major resources for clarifying this possibility are biblical texts. Their common use of biblical texts, particularly to explicate centripetal reading as moving toward an exit from the culture (Blanchot) and as abjection of the self (Kristeva), allows each of them to be compared with premodern theories of reading such as are gathered and redeployed by Calvin in his doctrine of Scripture. What they have in common with Calvin is that like him they read biblical texts as instructive first of all on the point crucial to this study, namely, how to read a text as scripture.

To follow Blanchot, Kristeva, and, keeping in mind the cultural distance, Calvin one must attend to reading and to reading the Bible as though for the first time, detached from the dominant cultural practices. To open up this possibility, I look at three matters. First, I point out various current, widespread, and powerful notions about the Bible that militate against the possibility of reading it as scripture. Next I indicate what it would mean to read biblical texts both centripetally, that is, toward cultural exit and abjection, and centrifugally, that is, toward a return of a speaking self to the culture. Finally, I address the very serious matter of biblical patriarchy, the question whether it is possible to read biblical texts as scripture when we have become so aware as we are now of biblical texts as hostages within the stout and powerfully guarded walls of political ideology.

I

There are several widespread and powerful assumptions that must be resisted if the Bible is to be read once again as scripture. Among them are some that have remarkable similarity to the alternatives Calvin rejected as he deployed his doctrine of reading Scripture. Just as Calvin opposed both the subjection of Bible reading to the church, on the one side, and the rejection of the "dead letter" of texts for an immediate relation to God claimed by spiritualists, on the other, so the prospect of reading the Bible as scripture is dependent on avoiding present-day versions of these Roman and Anabaptist alternatives. In order to be read as scripture the Bible must be freed from subjection both to new forms of institutionalism or communalism and new forms of spiritualism.

Today, as in Calvin's day, heavy claims on reading the Bible are made in the name of institutionalism and communalism. I have already noted adumbrations of such theories in the work of Stanley Fish, who argues that reading a text is a practice determined by the institutions, professional or communal, in which the text is engaged. Institutions, according to Fish, give the reader a sense of the text, of what is and what is not worth noting in it, and how it should be understood.

It is not at all surprising that theories of this kind have become powerful and productive in the discursive field of theologies. Their principal philosophical source is Wittgenstein and theories of "language games" or "forms of life" drawn particularly from his work. Basic to these theories is the recognition that communities develop their own particular languages and practices and that these are intelligible within those communities and not necessarily without. It follows that acts of reading, indeed all perceptions, are performed in specific contexts and on specific occasions by which they are conditioned. Norms legislated by or embodied within the practices of an institution govern reading and interpretation, and this is true not only for some but for all reading. The great appeal of this kind of theory is that it grants a new confidence to religious communities and confirms the force and significance of their languages and practices, since these must be seen in relation to particular institutional or communal situations. Since all communities have languages and practices, it can even be said that all languages and practices have their own "communities" and that there is nothing strange or unusual about the peculiar words and actions of religious communities. Religious communities no longer need think of themselves as exceptional in this regard, since no one reads anything without being located somewhere. The theological implications of this view of things has been nowhere more effectively spelled out than it was a decade or so ago by George Lindbeck in his widely influential book, *The Nature of Doctrine*.[1]

Another version of theological possibilities in this move is offered by Garrett Green,[2] and I turn to it because it leans more toward a perspectival than a communal emphasis, and I have already responded to the latter in my discussion of Fish and in my earlier response to Lindbeck. In addition, Green focuses on the role of "as" in his description of the situation of the reader, and "as" and "as if" have been recurring motifs in this study, since Calvin uses "sicut" strategically in his doctrines both of Scripture and of sacraments.

Green argues that people are always determined by understandings that allow them to see things in a certain way, to see them "as" this or that. He employs Wittgenstein to support a theory of the force and significance of religious language within the boundaries of communities defined by or identified with such language. Green implies that the doctrinal and institutional determinations of a church shape the practice of reading so that biblical texts are read in a certain way, for example, read "as" the word of God.

Green does not use "as," therefore, in a hypothetical or fictional sense, as it has been used by literary theories based on the work of Hans Vaihinger, such as Frank Kermode's. Kermode locates the "as" or "as if" wholly within the meaning-producing acts of the human mind, so that to read something "as if" grants no purchase on things as they actually are. Indeed, Kermode, borrowing from Vaihinger, postulates a contrary, if not contradictory, relation between things as they are and what we make of them; his position, like Vaihinger's, combines Hume and Kant.[3] Green, along with other religious thinkers or philosophers who argue along these lines, is not imputing to the perspective of the reader, determined as it is by location and beliefs, the source of textual coherence and significance. "As" is not "contrary to fact." Communal or perspectival emphases appear to be subjectivist only for those who continue to believe there is some place to stand that is apart from particular determinations and that grants direct access to actuality. However, while Green's use of "as" is not Vaihinger's or Kermode's, it is also not Calvin's.

Calvin uses "sicut" not to emphasize the location or perspective of the reader but to recognize the distance and the uncertainty that always exist between the reader and the saving knowledge that may be received in and by reading Scripture. The force of his locutions for both reading Scripture and receiving the sacrament is to block one from presuming that simply by reading one could achieve saving knowledge or that by taking the sacrament one could thereby receive the body of Christ. Following Saint Bernard and a whole tradition, he is relating the "sicut" to humility. His use of "as if" recognizes a line between what a reader can do and effect and the saving knowledge that can come to a reader in and through reading Scripture. The reader can go to that line but not any further; the reader can read in hope and faith, in an attitude of "as if"; and if saving knowledge is received, the reader knows that the ability to read in that way was also given and not self-generated.

Green's perspectival position and other such ways of construing reading will not lead to reading the Bible as scripture. These positions subject reading the Bible to perspectives and practices that arise from and are characteristic of the institution or occasion that forms reading's context. They are positions that subsume reading the Bible under a set of interests that determine how the Bible will be read, what it means to read the Bible "as . . ." While there is no question that reading can always be dominated by already formulated cognitive and institutional conclusions, it is precisely the possibility of delivery from such domination that reading the Bible as scripture holds out.

Although Green's position and others like it must not be taken as subjectivist or hypothetical, it is crucial to recognize the difference they hold from premodernist understandings of reading Scripture and from the theories of reading in Blanchot and Kristeva. Calvin's response to the stance of Green would be consistent with his attacks on the control by bishops of the practice of reading Scripture, on the imposition of their interests on it, and on their presumption of authority over how to read and over that to which reading would or could lead. Blanchot and Kristeva would add to Calvin the point that the important problem is not that which Green and those like him set out to address. The problem is not first of all how to have and to defend identity and coherence in the midst of a complex culture or to reach certainty in a culture of skepticism and antinomianism. The basic problem instead is how to give up positions and identities, even the positions and identities of critical detachment and iconoclasm, in a culture of possession and narcissism. The first question is how to give them up because there are no coherences or identities, even Christian ones, that are not obligated to the culture, even if only by contrast, and the self that desires to maintain them is a self that ignores the lacks, exclusions, and potential violence those coherences and identities conceal and is well on its way toward narcissism. The principal concern is not having a language game, a form of life, a coherence, a community, or a perspective but giving them up, divesting oneself of them, emptying one's hand, and dying to self and world "as though" or in the hope that a newness might arise. To read the Bible apart from that movement is not to read it as scripture, not to have been instructed in its principal directive—how it should be read.

That directive is indicated by the principal thrust of biblical narratives and exhortations. Calvin, like Blanchot and Kristeva, repeatedly illustrates, by reference to biblical texts, what it means to read; Kristeva, like Calvin, augments such references with appeals to theologians, such as Augustine and Bernard, as guides for this reading. They all consider the Bible as being first of all about how it should be read, and such a practice does not mean prosecuting one's perspective, confirming one's institution or coherence, or validating one's identity; it means instead the readiness to be delivered from and bereft of them.

This is not to say that institution and doctrine are unimportant. The question is one of relative status. Reading the Bible as scripture must lead to an exit from them. For theology this means, first of all, freeing reading from theological determinations, particularly the substitution of doctrines of scripture for reading the Bible. David Kelsey has shown convincingly how various Protestant theologies depend not so much on biblical texts as on a theology of the Bible that reading the Bible is designed to support.[4] This is not a practice isolated to conservative theologies; it covers the range. Similarly, Donald K. McKim surveys the uses of the Bible in diverse theological contexts and reveals how the Bible is used to grant certainty to theological formulations that are partial.[5] Indeed, a characteristic move of Christian theologies is to develop a coherent set of conclusions and to apply them to reading the Bible in order to confirm that coherence. Take the doctrine of God, for example. An understanding of God, even if derived from reading the Bible, becomes part of a theological coherence that is also culturally responsive to the criteria of intelligibility and adequacy. Then this doctrine of God is put into the sky, posited as real, and, Platonist-like, is thought to be manifest in various ways, including reading the Bible. The further tasks of the theology are to relate this extrapolated God to biblical texts, other aspects of theology, and human experience. In contrast, Calvin insists that we have no reliable understanding of God apart from the practice of reading Scripture. I would put the matter more simply: "God" is a word on a page, and coming to the recognition that it must be read, while no easy task, is the first step toward reading the Bible as scripture.

This is not to say that theology is unimportant. But its principal role is not to offer coherence and identity but, as it was for Calvin, to make better readers of Scripture. Theology, as it is in the *Institutes*, is first of all a guide and a response to reading the Bible as scripture. In addition, the principal formulations of theology should be, as they are in Calvin, illuminations and protections of the practice of reading the Bible as scripture. Finally, theology should expose its own tentative, partial, and incomplete state. In other words, theology should be the opposite of what it usually becomes.

Nor is all of this a way of discounting churches. But unity and stability in the church are not necessarily good things, and certainly imposed or abstract unity and stability are not. A church is first of all a community of scripture readers, a people engaged in the centripetal and centrifugal processes as they are taught them by biblical texts and theologies derived from them. The unity of the church is the unity of gratitude for church, selves, and worlds as temporary gifts. This unity will come to expression in doctrinal decisions and Christian labor, but there is much upon which members of a church will not and need not agree. And disagreement is less an obstacle to something good than the prevention of something bad, namely, the temptation to solidify the results of reading into something permanent, to use reading to certify what always must be brought into question. Given culture's tendencies toward narcissism, oppression, and polarization, group identity is not the problem; bringing it into question is the problem. Identity will begin to be questioned when churches, rather than conceal or fear partiality, incompleteness, and uncertainty, call them to attention and even foster them. Churches can then become not only communities of scripture readers but also places where reading the Bible as scripture can be recovered and retaught.

Having countered the domination of reading the Bible by institution and doctrine, I do not locate myself on the other side, among the spiritualists that Calvin opposed as much as he opposed the bishops' domination of reading. To reject notions derived from Wittgenstein—that reading the Bible should be subsumed under the auspices of the church or should be read to confirm or extend expectations derived from a coherence or identity—is not to place oneself on the other side with spiritualists who, in one form or another, suppose a relation of immediacy between the reader and the divine. As with Calvin, so today: spiritualist attitudes must be as fully eschewed as attitudes conditioned by institutional or cognitive coherence and interests, if the Bible is to be read as scripture.

A strong and in many ways attractive example of the spiritual understanding of reading a text as scripture is provided by M. Basil Pennington, who presents a deliberately detailed doctrine of reading the Bible as scripture. Pennington draws on many practices in the tradition of spiritual disciplines, including the *lectio divina*, and he is particularly influenced by Thomas Merton.[6] His use of *lectio divina* even leads him to advocate an exit from the confinements, certainties, and determinations of the culture and from the identities formed for and by it. There is much here, as there also is in Green's alternative position, to take seriously. But having said that, I must also point out that his assumptions are Platonist or spiritualist. He holds to an already certain continuity between the self and God that the discipline of reading can clarify or actualize. Imputed to this spiritual relation is an actuality that warrants the divestment of culture and of a former self because they now can be perceived as unreal and unreliable. Indeed, the discipline turns on a confidence not only in spiritual presence but in present time, and it posits entry into the present as a reality that stands in contrast to the temporal movement by which future turns into past. Assumed is a spiritual center or beginning in which the reader already, although not aware of it, participates and which, by reading, is gradually disclosed and made conscious.

Another set of spiritualist understandings of reading lie in the direction, taken by a number of postmodernist theologians, of exit from the culture into some place outside. It is a position that advocates nomadism outside the walls of culture and the confinements of identity as a way of life, that takes textual and reading theory as a way of getting outside and staying there. A good example of spiritualism of this kind is offered in the work of Mark C. Taylor.[7] To advocates of this new nomadism Blanchot and Kristeva would respond that while culture and self can be divested and abjected, there also must be a return, however much the culture and the self are altered in the return.

A final form, far less sophisticated than the above but more pervasive these days, is the use of locutions, across denominational lines, by evangelical and similar Christians, that exchange reading the Bible for a "personal relation to Christ." Calvin would say to such people that there we have no Christ, and no Holy Spirit, and no relation with them apart from reading Scripture.

I come now, however, to a difficult point. Previously I remarked on the distance between Calvin's culture and our own due to its Platonism and assumptions about the transcendent that it allowed him to share with others. We do not as a culture share such assumptions. It could be argued that Calvin advocated such radical and risky notions of reading because the culture was largely stabilized by shared belief in transcendent reality. Without such support, can such a theory of reading be recovered and redeployed? Without a sustaining cultural Platonism, can and will reading of this kind be undertaken?

We can ask this question first of Kristeva. Her answer has two sides. One considers the state of unworkability characteristic of the analysand's self. The clinical situation is created out of desperation and impasse. In addition, the analyst in the psychotherapeutic context, by means of transference, allows a love relation to emerge with the analysand that can sustain the client when passage is made from the abjection of a self to the self's reconstitution. This answer is supported by a considerable amount of theory on the primacy of personal relations, particularly derived from the work of Levinas. Primary relations are posited as sustaining to and not exhausted by language, culture, and identities. This first answer should not be dismissed. It is too real and well documented to discount. People have come out of terribly limiting, disabling, and destructive identities and behaviors by processes in which acceptance, forgiveness, and love formed a sustaining context. But it is not a fully reassuring answer. For one thing it slips too easily into sentimentality, a form of spiritualism, or a romantic humanism. More important, it is too occasional, too dependent on the contributions made to the reader by the presence of other persons. I see this as a powerful and important answer but as a partial one, therefore. Human relations are also dissolved by reading the Bible as scripture.

Blanchot takes us further, I think. His principal answer is a negative one. The reader simply can no longer be associated with the daylight world, with the culture of violence, accumulation, and visibility. The self formed by this culture can also no longer be endured. Anything, even nothing, is better than these identities, coherences, and certainties. One reads, then, with no expectation of anything, but one reads anyway because the alternative is not any longer possible. This is more like Calvin and the tradition upon which he drew, a tradition that recognizes both in one's world and self evil that can no longer be borne. Even more so than with Kristeva I would say that there is much here that satisfies as an answer to the question, but I also think that it is not adequate. It is not because it is too exceptional a state to posit as a cultural practice. True, many come to a point of renunciation of self and culture, and all of us have known more or less deep recognitions of a sickeningly questionable world or self. But this wholly negative way of accounting for the practice of reading the Bible as scripture, while I would go far with it, seems only to apply to some people or to others only partly.

A third factor needs to be added to the answers of Kristeva and Blanchot, and it is an answer derived from Calvin's use of the "sicut." It is a recognition of gap or barrier, to be sure. For Calvin, this gap or barrier needs always to be recognized because the reader comes to the end of reading still not in a position for moral reasons to make claims on God. Even reading does not give the reader chips that, at the end of the process, can be cashed in for saving knowledge. But for us the problem is more cognitive. We read, divest, and abject also "as if," but ours is more of a cognitive "as if," a recognition that our ideas, expectations, or desires for God, like the morality of deeds for Calvin, have no leverage whatsoever. Uncertainty is so radical and thorough at the end of reading that it disengages us from the mutual holds that culture and self have on us and we on them. The "as if" is a cognitive humility, but it also has moral consequences. For in a culture in which power is dissociated from the restraints of shared values, power takes to itself, as Blanchot points out, the certainty denied those values. The initial, basic moral consequence of reading the Bible as scripture is to deprive power, and its use, of the cognitive certainty that it otherwise takes to itself.

II

Having now released reading the Bible both from institutional or theological determinations and from the lures of spiritual immediacies, we can go on to reject practices of reading the Bible that are so well established as to be taken as unavoidable and natural. The Bible commonly is read first of all for its content, and the principal form reading takes is interpretation and appropriation. But reading the Bible as scripture involves first of all movement away from self and world and toward their divestment and abjection. In centripetal reading the coherences and identities of the reader and the reader's situation are dissolved, and biblical coherences and identities, rather than be appropriated, are followed as indicators of an exit and then bypassed on the way to it. The reader accompanies biblical characters who leave the security of their homes and venture into forbidding uncertainties; the reader "walks," as Calvin liked to say, with the patriarchs away from cultural identities and locations or, like Job, past the theological certainties of culture's representatives in order to stand divested even of the questions that subvert the adequacy of biblical theologies. Biblical locations, plots, characters, and theological themes, when taken as directives toward this kind of reading, are invaluable and authoritative because they clarify the act of divestment and abjection, of departure and exit, and because they ask to be left behind.

Centripetal reading is a process that leads to the divestment not only of one's world and sense of self but of biblical worlds and identities as well. It is a matter of first accompanying and then going on alone. However, the significance and force of the biblical material itself in leading the reader in the process of divestment and in releasing the reader to go on alone should not be underestimated. As I have said, what is so powerful about the theories of reading in Calvin and Blanchot and Kristeva is that their theories arise from or find ready confirmation in biblical texts. Blanchot refers constantly to the patriarchs, and he remarks the willingness of Abraham to leave the security of his familiar home and to go to a place not only where he has never been but about which he knows nothing. Similarly, Abraham is prepared to go to a place where he is to offer as sacrifice his only son, his future, the text, so to speak, of his expectations. Other moments in the sagas of the patriarchs are also important, such as Jacob's nighttime venture to wrestle with the border guardian at the Jabbok Brook. As a result of that encounter, Jacob receives, along with his name, or identity, a wounded hip, a chronic instability.

The Exodus narrative also points in the direction of centripetal reading. The people are led from the securities of Egypt into the hardships and uncertainties of the wilderness. And the Exodus is related both to the exile into Babylon and to the return of some of the people to the devastated land after the exile is lifted. These journeys are all exchanges of the certain and secure for the uncertain and forbidding.

The prophets of the Hebrew Bible also direct the people away from the securities and comforts provided by political and social structures and toward a way of life marked by uncertainty. For several of the prophets, beginning with Elijah, the wilderness, with all its uncertainty, provides a more fitting place for the people than do the securities of settled cultures in agrarian and urban Judah and Israel. Micah and Jeremiah take their attack on the sources of security and certainty to the very precincts of the temple, the heart of the people's religious life. Their denunciations of stability and confidence could not be stronger.

Job, an important text for Calvin, traces what I have called the bypassing of theologies. Job tenaciously persists in his refusal to accept the theological points of his culture's spokesmen, risking their judgment not only for what he may have done in the past but for the impiety of his present course of questions. Once outside the answers and categories theologies provide, Job finds himself called on to abject the very process of insistence and interrogation that carried him beyond the categories definitive of his culture and its understandings of self. Even the path of bypassing must be disowned and divested.

The Gospels no less indicate the process of centripetal reading. They are structured by the journey of Jesus to Jerusalem, which is a center not of certainty and triumph but of death and dispersal. And the reader, like the disciples, is enjoined to leave all behind and to follow, not simply to see what will happen or to draw moral and theological conclusions but also to die. Indeed, I have tried to argue that Mark, which can be taken as the first of the Gospels to have been written, is a journey narrative that allows readers to go to Jerusalem in order to die without having to make a physical journey that, for people distant from the place itself, would be out of the question for physical and political, if not also economic, reasons.[8]

Julia Kristeva points to Paul as one in whom the abject most fully has become coincident with oneself. Paul was, for Calvin, a constant guide to what it might mean to read the Bible as scripture, because Paul emphasizes the process of self-emptying and the dissociation of the divine from what is culturally secured as worthy of merit and praise.

The proposal that in centripetal reading not only the theologies and identities of the reader but also those encountered in the Bible are bypassed and left behind for the sake of the exit is not so new as at first it may sound. Readers of the Bible have always had to bypass what is culturally specific and for that reason as well as others inapplicable to their own situation. Calvin was explicit about the cultural confinements of biblical materials, and his theory of accommodation can be extended to encompass all of the Bible as culturally specific and limited.

In addition, the doctrine of accommodation applies to the whole of the Bible also by virtue of Calvin's understanding of biblical language. His doctrine of accommodation is related to his theory of centripetal reading because biblical language prevents the reader from ascending to knowledge of God. Biblical language requires humility and offends the finer senses of the reader and notions of how the reader deserves to be addressed. What Calvin calls saving knowledge of God is not, for him, received by acquisition, gradual ascent, or slow but sure improvement. It requires divestment, emptying, or dying to self and world. It is a process like that which he describes under the topic of repentance.

However, centripetal reading is only one aspect of reading the Bible as scripture. The exit is also a cul-de-sac, and return means a reconstitution of self and of one's world. Once divestment and abjection occur, centrifugal reading begins. And it is by language one returns, for language, although changed, reappears, as does the morning for Blanchot's insomniac. However, centrifugal reading does not repress the night or the exit; it takes them along and is conditioned by the uncertainty they impart. As did Jacob from the encounter at the Jabbok Brook with the night visitor, so the reader emerges from the exit not only with a limp, a chronic instability, but also with a new name, a changed identity, and world.

It is important to emphasize that reading the Bible as scripture produces not only a chronic instability but also a new identity, because so much postmodernist thought and deconstructive strategy opposes identity and even posits the outside, the wilderness, the nomadic, the incoherent, and the uncentered as a place where one can be located. As I noted, such assumptions constitute a form of spiritualism, an illusion that one can live outside of culture and without an identity. This error, as I have suggested, is as grave as that of institutionalists or communalists for whom transcendence is the lateral removal to a privileged, separated place. While centripetal reading opposes primarily the institutionalist error, centrifugal reading opposes primarily the error of forms of spiritualism that make refusal to return a possibility. As one leaves institution and identity behind in centripetal reading, one leaves exit and wilderness behind in centrifugal. Although uneasy with and uncertain about coherence and identity and aware of the fact that they are taken up by excluding others, even at others' expense and suffering, one takes them up again, although in altered form. So I am faced again with being a white male American academic professional—to use Zorba's words, "the whole catastrophe." Not only are these lamentable, however; they are also received as occasions of reconstitution. The challenge of centrifugal reading is to allow these identities so to be marked by exit that they do not become idols or "abiding cities" but departure points from which journeys to exits are constantly launched. For centrifugal reading, the challenge is to allow these identities and coherences to be taken up in a nonidolatrous and nonlethal way—knowing, however, that they will always become idolatrous and lethal again.

Here the Bible also serves as a model for reading a text as scripture, for it suggests the kinds of consequences that arise from the exit. One is apodictic. The reader emerges from the wilderness and from abjection with a clearer and sharper set of distinctions between what is and is not good. As one returns to the culture after psychotherapeutic healing knowing that this or that must at all costs be avoided and that this or that must receive the attention and confirmation it deserves, so the centrifugal reader emerges with a sharper sense of distinctions between what is beneficial and what harmful, what worthy of attention and what not. To draw a milder analogy, one returns from a vacation with a less confused view of the workplace and resolves not to let a troublesome colleague be a bother, to take up neglected or difficult tasks, or not to allow anxiety to build up.

There are also conditional distinctions by which things are weighed and evaluated not so much in an unambiguous way as in relation to one another. New combinations and separations, new priorities and alignments, and new social and political strategies arise. Like the laws promulgated at the gate or like the directives Paul gives to the churches for responding to problems, these are ways of making the best of things. One allows an ongoing, workable arrangement and style of operating to emerge.

Because ethics in the modern period is so much an enterprise tied to cognitive certainty, it may be difficult to accept the suggestion that ethics or morality, in these apodictic and conditional forms, can arise from so radical a sense of uncertainty as I have attached to centripetal reading. Crucial to this proposal is a sense of the moral dangers that inhere in cognitive certainty, in certainty about identity, coherence, world, and judgment. And while certainty is always a threat to reading the Bible as scripture, it is also a threat to living the moral life, and nothing is more threatening to both than theological certainty. When the grip of certainty on self and world are dissolved in centripetal reading, moral identity and a more reliable form of deportment within one's world emerge.

A final consequence of centrifugal reading is what I call normalization. One returns to self and world not only with a changed and clearer set of moral distinctions and value judgments but also with a new form of world affirmation. This is the normality to which Job returns after his extremities. Here all of the biblical language about contentment and gratitude comes into play.

Normalization is possible only in an attitude of uncertainty, of nonpossession and noninsistence. Receiving a world uncertainly can be described as humility and gratitude, but it is not a form of weakness or confusion. It is an attitude of not taking anything as more or other than it is, namely, partial and tentative. The restored and returned are affirmed not despite, but because of, the fact that they are not complete and permanent. They are not taken as more or other than they are.

A sense of normalization as gift is suggested by Peter De Vries in his novel *The Blood of the Lamb.* The narrative, which is largely based on the story of his own daughter's death, recounts the relation of a father to his daughter during her protracted struggle with leukemia. During that struggle, there are periods of remission, and the narrator reflects on the kind of swelling of normality that these periods of remission provide. Nothing is so rich and so meaningful as the everyday when it has been returned after having been threatened or taken away. This sense of gratitude at having the normal returned does not depend on an illusion of the normal's permanence. Both father and daughter know that the stay is temporary, the return partial. But the affirmation of the normal, of a world restored, is no less strong for that. Such normalization depends on uncertainty and impermanence. Returning to the normal is not settling in, not taking things for granted. It is a reception of the world and self, in their ambiguities, as tentative gifts.

Cultural, group, and personal identities do not remain gifts for long. They soon become burdens and weapons that must again be divested and abjected. One indication of this change is that a person begins to take the world, first, for granted, then as something to be retained, and finally as a possession to be protected and enlarged. One begins to relate to it out of need, to depend upon it, and to defend it. This process is inevitable and gives rise to the need again for centripetal reading. That need becomes recognizable in what Kristeva calls narcissism and what Blanchot calls the violence of culture. I would also like to add that it becomes recognizable in polarization. Polarization may be mistaken for the consequence of centripetal reading because polarization sets persons or groups against one another, and when the other is taken as a large part of society or culture, opposition or alienation may appear as part of the discipline of exit. But polarization is a radical form of identity clarification and validation, and as such it is wholly contained within the dynamics of the culture. Its most common form is negative, and it occurs both in individual and in group identities. Kristeva discusses a fascinating way in which the structures of youthful erotic relations are established by polarization. Using Romeo and Juliet as example, she describes how people come into a sense of close relationship by opposing the world around them. The world as other is seen negatively, and it is from defiance of it that the content of the relationship is derived.[9] Indeed, teenagers, who have very few resources from which to develop relationships positively, typically create them in this negative fashion, developing intimacy by means of rejecting or denigrating the rest of society, particularly its power and authority. But this pattern extends further than such moments in adolescent development. It is a common ingredient in the formation of individual and group identity. Indeed, identity formation is very hard to distinguish from the dynamics of polarization. The less positive content there is to the formation of identity, that is, the less "normality" (as described above), the more identity begins to depend on and be reduced to polarization.

Narcissism, certainty, and polarization are all potential forms of violence because they impute autonomy and finality to what is partial, contingent, and mutually implicated. They are all forms or results of abstraction. They mark a situation in which reading has ended and been exchanged for appropriation, enlargement, and validation. Narcissism, certainty, and polarization provide the principal shape and dynamic of a culture without the reading of texts as scripture, and from the vantage point of academia they seem now and for a long while to come the only games in town.

III

Finally, returning to the difficult question whether the Bible can be read as scripture now that the extent and the consequences of patriarchy in these texts have been laid bare, I would like to propose that biblical patriarchy actually may help us to recognize what reading the Bible as scripture would be like. In making this proposal I turn to Calvin's doctrine of accommodation and, more important, to Calvin's use of biblically described idolatry within the context of his doctrine of reading Scripture.

First, I must point out that patriarchy is only the latest in a series of obstacles posed for readers of biblical texts by the limits and particularities of the cultures in which they arose. These obstacles Calvin treated under the rubric of accommodation, and he implied that the reader need not be confined by those cultural particularities but could move out from under them in what I have been calling centrifugal reading. Like other features of biblical texts—laws concerning daily commerce, social practices, or cosmology—patriarchy is yet another reason why reading the Bible is not a matter of simply leaving one's own culture to enter biblical culture or re-creating biblical culture alongside the contemporary world.

Biblical patriarchy, however much as it stands with other culturally conditioned aspects of biblical texts to keep us from directly appropriating them, differs from previous obstacles to biblical appropriation. It is different first of all by reason of its pervasiveness. The cosmology of the ancient Near East can be bracketed as noticeably relevant to only some biblical texts, such as the Creation and flood stories, many of the Psalms, or the ascension of Jesus in Acts 1. But patriarchy touches every page, indeed, every sentence of the Bible. Indirectly or directly, virtually all the language of biblical texts carries the marks of patriarchy. One has to deal with it all the time, whereas there are many parts of the Bible from which ancient cosmology fades or for which it needs not be taken into account.

Furthermore, biblical cosmology is not an evil. While it is related to biblical ideas about evil and while it may have had some evil consequences, especially when neighboring peoples were related to flood waters that needed to be pushed back for a land to appear, one can think of a cosmology as fairly neutral. But patriarchy is evil. I do not only mean that patriarchy is evil because it represents a cultural, social, political, and economic system in which women are subservient to men and some women subservient to other women, although I do not want to underestimate evil of that kind. Indeed, since one could say that all social and political structures are in some ways and to some degree evil and need regularly and radically to be interrogated or even opposed, one cannot call biblical patriarchy exceptional simply because its social and political arrangements and consequences are evil in this sense. Rather, biblical patriarchy is evil because it presents a strong obstacle to and temptation from reading the text as though it were scripture. In other words, it is idolatrous.

One of the reasons why people do not read the Bible centripetally, why they do not bypass its culturally or theologically specific locations and identities, why they want to settle for the meaning of the text as an appropriation or confirmation rather than divest themselves of certainty is that they have an interest in and addiction to biblical patriarchy. Biblical hermeneutics, throughout Christian history and down to its most recent manifestations, cannot be separated from the lure of this song. Whenever reading the Bible has been taken to mean not a process of self- and world-abjection but a process of appropriating biblical meaning and applying it to today's world, biblical patriarchy, because it touches virtually every word of the texts, is assimilated, along with the idolatry it represents, and is perpetuated.

Just as Calvin included a section on idolatry in his doctrine of reading Scripture, so is it necessary today to address idolatry in a theory of reading the Bible as scripture because one of the appeals of the Bible is the idolatry of patriarchy. What is necessary is to extend Calvin's notion of human nature as a "factory of idols" beyond the biblical moments he highlighted, such as the people's reversion to the idol while Moses ascended Mount Sinai, to include virtually every word. Why is this called for?

The principal conditions of human life as recounted in biblical texts are uncertainty, change, dislocation, and cultural trauma. The amazing thing is that the people carry on in the face of and despite these conditions, ostensibly because God is not identified with a particular configuration and is not compromised when a cultural situation is changed or lost. Indeed, an, if not *the*, central affirmation concerning God is that while all social and political structures and continuities are uncertain and unreliable, including, for some, the people themselves, God is faithful, constant, and unrelenting of purpose. God is reliable even though events, people, and cultures are not. But the texts also affirm that something else survives or transcends cultural change and political uncertainty, namely, patriarchy. It is not only God who is able to provide continuity and stability in the face of radical and even violent changes in the lives of people; patriarchy also remains stable, reliable, constant, and certain. For the biblical texts, then, what abides, what transcends change, is not only (or perhaps not so much) God but patriarchy. Its constancy and stability provide assurance and recompense in the face of trauma and loss.

Since idolatry is the attribution of deity to something cultural, the mistaking of God for something that grants certainty to world and self, then the

Bible is not only complicated or compromised by idolatry, it is also a ready source of it. While the question whether the Bible can be read as though it were scripture is a question severely taxed by biblical patriarchy, biblical patriarchy also clarifies what reading the Bible as scripture might be like, for now one cannot pause at any point along the way toward an exit, cannot rest with any biblical formulations. Not only are those formulations often irrelevant or inapplicable to our own time, they are also complicitous in cultural idolatry. When one reads the Bible as scripture, then, one needs to read against the grain not of a part but of the whole of it.

Women who read the Bible have been for some time now aware of this situation. Rosemary Radford Ruether writes, for example, "Patriarchy itself must fall under the Biblical denunciations of idolatry and blasphemy, the idolizing of the male as representative of divinity. It is idolatrous to make males more 'like God' than females. It is blasphemous to use the image and name of the Holy to justify patriarchal domination and law. Feminist readings of the Bible can discern a norm within Biblical faith by which the Biblical texts themselves can be criticized."[10] But her position, while powerful, pits one part of the Bible, especially the prophets, against other parts, as though the prophetic material is not (or is less) patriarchal. But this kind of abstraction of a biblical principle from the texts is idealist. A principle, I would argue, cannot be dissociated from its situation. Indeed, Ruether's move, while extreme, is not different from the whole of the hermeneutical enterprise, down to its contemporary representatives: it is a process of extracting meaning from the cultural shell or husk of the text. Indeed, while I would say that for Calvin a saving knowledge of God is not a principle that the reader extracts from the text but a situation one enters or is brought into, even Calvin, working under the influence of a determining theo-philosophical tradition, may not be free from the idolatries of that tradition. The only way they can be avoided is through the bypassing that centripetal reading requires. The text is no abiding place, and it cannot be appropriated or interpreted unless the reader has first passed through the text to an exit. The clearest indicators of the direction toward exit may be biblical women.

Alicia Suskin Ostriker suggests how biblical women help to illuminate the way toward exit, what I call centripetal reading. She points to biblical subplots or subtexts by which women, as in the patriarchal stories, are gradually excluded from the text.[11] Women end up on the outside or are forgotten. Even when they have a place and role in a story, that role and place are partial, temporary, and uncertain. The women make exits or are rejected. This means that the stories of women in the Bible more fully indicate what it would be like to read the Bible as though it were scripture than do the stories of men. Abraham becomes more and more situated and confirmed; Sarah gradually exits. It is Sarah, then, who traces the path of the centripetal reader, with whom, as Calvin said of Abraham and the other patriarchs, the reader should walk.

The Kristeva supplement should not, however, be forgotten. Feminist theology and feminist biblical hermeneutics emphasize deliverance as getting out from under an oppressive, external force; they stand, with this emphasis, more with Blanchot and his attention to the culture out from under which his exit leads than with Kristeva. Feminist and other liberation theologies stress deliverance from external enemies. However, the centripetal reading of a text as scripture includes deliverance from one's self as well. To include this side of centripetal reading may seem like "attacking the victim," but it need not; the self that becomes abject is also formed by the culture, and if that culture is recognized as oppressive or distorting, the self, even the self as victim, can and should be left behind by centripetal reading.

Feminist theory and other critical assessments of identity construction in our culture indicate how important the act of exiting is. The status and role of the woman, as they have been constructed by modern ideologies especially since the beginning of the nineteenth century, need radically to be brought into question. For that reason as well, all identities, including that of white males, are complicitous in a culture that has turned identity construction into a lethal practice. Consequently, feminist reading is in a position to indicate, along with other voices that register the consequences of modernist identity formation, how important it is to divest oneself of those constructions before the activity of reconstructing a female—or any—identity can commence. Indeed, it is in and by the process of divestment that one begins to realize how absolutely vital or life-giving it can be. What needs further to be said is that cultural representations of the self have been internalized and are not simply alien, external constraints. This means that the process of centripetal reading cannot be simply the rejection of a culture's representations but also must be an abjection of the self that these constructions have produced. Finally, it must also be said that the reader, having given herself to this divestment and abjection, cannot remain shorn and relieved but must return to the culture, one in which she will have, again, to take up the question, in a process I have been calling centrifugal reading, of what it shall now mean to be a woman, what will go into the reconstitution of that now always tentative and partial identity formation. Minorities and others who have similarly suffered will recognize the need and possibilities of following these indicators, and last but not least the principal constructors of lethal representations of others may be able themselves to recognize how most of all it is they who need to follow, to divest and abject this habit and to return to the culture freed from its addictive powers.

NOTES

Chapter 1

1. For support, see A. Mitchell Hunter, *The Teaching of Calvin: A Modern Interpretation* (London: James Clarke & Co., 1950), 69.

2. "[T]he intellectual and cultural resources available to thinkers of the sixteenth century made the production of 'systematic thought' almost inconceivable." William J. Bouwsma, *John Calvin: A Sixteenth-Century Portrait* (New York: Oxford University Press, 1988), 5.

3. Ibid., 32. One wonders, from statements like this and like that in the preceding footnote, if Bouwsma has put more twentieth-century characteristics into the sixteenth than that culture could itself muster.

4. "Since, therefore, men one and all perceived that there is a God and that he is their Maker, they are condemned by their own testimony because they have failed to honor him and to consecrate their lives to his will." Calvin *Institutes* 1.3.1.

5. Calvin's principal adversary on the matter of taking the Bible seriously enough, of course, was the Church, which tended to subsume Scripture to its own authority.

6. "It was on Easter Day 1538 that he had stopped, and September 1541 when he went on to the next verse as if it were only the following day. From this, however, it is clear that his sermons were already expository and, it would seem, already connected series on whole books of the Bible." "He began at chapter one verse one of a book and continued with one or a few or many verses for each sermon until he had got to the end of that book. The next day or the next Sunday he started on another book." "[For Calvin] . . . preaching must conform to Scripture. It is the humble position of preaching as derivative and subordinate that is precisely its glory." T.H.L. Parker, *Calvin's Preaching* (Louisville, Ky.: Westminster/John Knox Press, 1992), 60, 63, and 23. This homiletic mode was not an invention of Calvin or the Reformers. It represents a selection or emphasis from a tradition that goes back to the fathers and was clarified and organized by Gregory the Great. See Rosamond McKitterick, *The Frankish Church and the Carolingian Reforms, 789–895* (Cambridge: Cambridge University Press, 1978), 6:86–93.

7. *Institutes* 1.6.1 and 1.14.1.

8. See Lawrence G. Duggan, "Was Art Really the 'Book of the Illiterate'?" *Word & Image* 5, no. 3 (1989): 227–51, and Celia M. Chazelle, "Pictures, Books, and the Illiterate: Pope Gregory I's Letters to Serenus of Marseilles," *Word & Image* 6, no. 2 (1990): 138–52.

9. *Institutes* 1.11.5.

10. Calvin's extension of the reading of Scripture to include all Christians despite their social standing does not mean that Calvin favored removing all social distinctions. "He did not believe therefore that the rich should share with the poor to the extent of banishing the distinction between them. But though he believed in the necessity of some distinctions remaining, he believed that the appearance of extreme differences in wealth and poverty within a community was inexcusably evil." Ronald S. Wallace, *Calvin, Geneva, and the Reformation: A Study of Calvin as Social Reformer, Churchman, Pastor, and Theologian* (Edinburgh: Scottish Academic Press, 1988), 93. "Calvin's emphasis on the importance of social differentiation for the maintenance of order is one source of his doctrine of the calling. The calling to which every human being has been assigned by God was for him a kind of earthly equivalent of the orbit of a heavenly body. . . . Calling stabilized the social order." Bouwsma, *John Calvin*, 74.

11. An excellent and readable description of the origins, development, and importance of *lectio divina* in Benedict and monastic life can be found in Norvene West, *No Moment Too Small: Rhythms of Silence, Prayer, and Holy Reading*, Cicercian Studies Series, no. 153 (Kalamazoo, Mich.: Cicercian Publications, 1994); see esp. "Holy Reading," 59–86. However, this discussion moves too easily, in my view, from the discipline of reading to the elaboration, especially in terms of the fourfold hermeneutic, of the text's meanings. My reasons for this demurral become clearer later.

12. Jean Leclercq, O.S.B., *The Love of Learning and the Desire for God: A Study of Monastic Culture*, trans. Catharine Misrahi (New York: Fordham University Press, 1961), 90.

13. "This means that the most intimate concepts of Scripture are not addressed to the 'rational' intellect, but to an understanding derived from 'taste'—spiritual, living, and feeding our souls." Peter Norber, S.J., "Lectio Vere Divina: St. Bernard and the Bible," *Monastic Studies*, no. 3 (1965): 174; see generally 165–81.

14. Roger Corless, "Authority (2): An Essay on the Place of the Text in Buddhist and Christian Formation," *Studies in Formative Spirituality* 14, no. 1 (1993): 36.

15. "The College de Montaigu appears to have been in the forefront of this nominalist revival in the first decades of the sixteenth century. Calvin thus attended a college at which the influence of the *via moderna* appears to have been unquestioned." Alister E. McGrath, *A Life of John Calvin: A Study in the Shaping of Western Culture* (Oxford: Basil Blackwell, 1990), 42.

16. Ibid., 43–45.

17. Ibid., 56.

18. See, for example, *Institutes* 3.15.4.

19. "An influential characteristic of 'Calvinism' which we undoubtedly find in Calvin himself was a desire for simplicity. In his own life-style he preferred plainness (in the good sense of that word) to any kind of unnecessary elaboration." Wallace, *Calvin, Geneva, and the Reformation*, 281.

20. "Between 1527 and 1534 . . . Calvin inhabited the Erasmian world of thought and breathed its spiritual atmosphere; he remained in major ways always a humanist of the late Renaissance." Bouwsma, *John Calvin*, 13. See also Wallace, *Calvin, Geneva, and the Reformation*.

21. *The Handbook of the Christian Soldier* (Enchiridion militis christiani), trans. Charles Fantazzi, in *Collected Works of Erasmus*, ed. John W. O'Malley (Toronto: University of Toronto Press, 1988), 66:34, 35.

22. See Herman Hailperin, *Rashi and the Christian Scholars* (Pittsburgh, Pa.: University of Pittsburgh Press, 1963), 137–246.

23. *Institutes* 1.7.1, 1.9.1.

24. *Institutes* 1.8.2, 1.13.1.

25. "Thereupon his powers are mentioned, by which he is shown to us not as he is in himself, but as he is toward us: so that this recognition of him consists more in living experience than in vain and high-flown speculation." *Institutes* 1.10.2. "[For Calvin] God has no commerce with men apart from Scripture." Parker, *Calvin's Preaching*, 4.

26. "Renaissance humanists rejected Scholastic education, which depended primarily on logic, the act of organizing truth into rationally intelligible systems of thought, and turned instead to rhetoric, the art of persuasion. . . . Their preference for persuasion over rational conviction was associated with a view of human beings as passionate, active and social rather than intellectual." Bouwsma, *John Calvin*, 114.

27. *Institutes* 1.8.2.

28. *Institutes* 2.3.8.

29. Many interpreters of Calvin see this as a part of his understanding of the Christian life, but they do not identify its principal and proper place as in the act of reading. So, for example, Ronald S. Wallace says, "Nothing must be omitted from the totality of the sacrifice. Every aspect, attitude, love, prize, habit of the old self must be brought to the altar and slain." *Calvin, Geneva, and the Reformation*, 190. While this is generally true for Calvin, it is true for him because it is first of all descriptive of what it means to read Scripture as if there the living word of God were to be heard.

30. See Norber, "Lectio Vere Divina."

31. *Institutes* 1.6.1.

32. At pivotal moments, such as that in which he discusses the process of divestment that must precede the reception of grace, Calvin often draws on Augustine or Bernard. A typical example is *Institutes* 3.12.8.

33. In addition, Beryl Smalley traces the *lectio divina* back to Saint Augustine. See his *Study of the Bible in the Middle Ages* (Oxford: Basil Blackwell, 1952), 29.

34. Bernard of Clairvaux, *De Gradibus Humilitatis et Superbiae*, ed. Barton R. V. Mills (Cambridge: Cambridge University Press, Cambridge Patristic Texts, 1926); see esp. 102–3 and 154. The treatise on humility and pride is based, in the first part, on the twelve degrees of humility that are enumerated in the seventh chapter of Saint Benedict's "Rule." The discussion of pride in terms of twelve corresponding degrees is Bernard's invention.

35. "Augustine's *City of God* was the most popular. . . . St. Bernard's works of mysticism were often reprinted too." Lucien Febvre and Henri-Jean Martin, *The Coming of the Book: The Impact of Printing, 1450–1800*, trans. David Gerard (London: NLB, 1976), 251; see also 287. It is interesting to notice how Calvin conformed to the tastes of his day. Febvre and Martin also point out that the printed book can be said to have arrived during the first decade of the sixteenth century (262), that Seneca was extremely popular, and that the principal purchasers of books in Paris during the opening decades of the century were lawyers rather than clergymen. While it would not do to deny Calvin's originality, it can also be said that he rode a wave not only in terms of the rising importance of printed books, which, by the middle of the century had displaced manuscripts (262), but also in terms of the religious tastes of the day. Calvin's stress on the religious importance of reading for each Christian, his emphasis on the Bible, which, of course, in translations was the best seller of the century, and his use of theologians well known to many readers all served to make Calvin's own books, by midcentury, best-sellers, too.

36. *Institutes* 1.7.1.

37. "In attempting to establish equity between both the Old and the New Testament, Calvin's theology was the least inequitable or anti-Judaic of the major classical theological systems." Calvin Augustine Pater, "Calvin, the Jews, and the Judaic Legacy," in *In Honor of John Calvin, 1509–64*, Papers for the 1986 International Calvin Symposium, McGill University, ed. E. J. Furcha (Montreal: McGill University Press, 1987) , 290–91; see generally 256–95. Pater goes

on to say that when Calvin argues against Judaism, it is not against the Law itself but against legalism and ceremonialism, and Calvin saw more of that in papal Christianity than in Judaism.

38. Joseph Haroutunian, ed., commentary on 1 Cor. 10:11, in *Calvin: Commentaries* (Louisville, Ky.: Westminster/John Knox Press, Library of Christian Classics, 1979), 92. See also commentaries on Jer. 26:4–5, p. 82, and on Acts 7:38, pp. 103–4.

39. Human nature he calls a factory of idols. *Institutes* 1.11.8.

40. Commentary on 2 Cor. 3:6–10, in *Calvin: Commentaries*, 107.

41. Commentary on John 5:39, in ibid., 104.

42. "Calvin certainly believed that as people came close to Christ together in heart and living communion they would begin to find their doctrinal differences becoming less." Wallace, *Calvin, Geneva, and the Reformation*, 148.

43. "Against the objection that if everyone has a right to be a judge and arbiter concerning the truths of the Bible, nothing can be 'set down as certain, and our whole religion will be full of uncertainty,' I reply that we must test doctrine in a twofold way: private and public. By private testing, each one establishes his own faith, and accepting only the teaching which he knows to be from God. For our conscience cannot find security and peace except in God. Public testing of doctrine has to do with the consent and polity of the church." Commentary on 1 John 4:1, in *Calvin: Commentaries*, 87.

44. He also noted that participants in these councils were not in agreement on all details or on the use and meaning of the language of conclusions. See, for example, *Institutes* 1.13.5.

45. "Since there is a danger that fanatical men may rise up and boast rashly that they have the Spirit of God, believers should seek a remedy by coming together and reasoning their way to an honest and godly agreement. . . . therefore, it is a marvelous work of God that, overcoming all our perversity, he makes us of one mind, and unites us together in a pure unity of faith." Commentary on 1 John 4:1, in *Calvin's Commentaries*, 88.

46. On the latter, see Bouwsma, *John Calvin*, 138.

47. Calvin is eager that nonessential matters not become bases for schisms in the church. See *Institutes* 4.1.12.

48. John H. Leith, *An Introduction to the Reformed Tradition* (Atlanta: John Knox Press, 1978), 98 (emphasis added).

49. Notice how much Calvin's extended discussion of the doctrine of repentance resembles the attitude toward reading that is implied in his doctrine of Scripture. *Institutes* 3.3.5.

50. For example, see the commentary on John 3:12, in *Calvin's Commentaries*, 90.

51. Parker, *Calvin's Preaching*, 23.

52. "Calvinism was often regarded as progressive, associated in many minds with a decisive break with obsolete institutions, customs and practices fettering individuals to the legacy of the feudal past. Where Luther seemed cautious and conservative, Calvin appeared bold and forward-looking." McGrath, *A Life of John Calvin*, 199.

Chapter 2

1. This passage from the second article of the Belgic Confession, by incorporating the trope of reading nature not only as a book but as a second scripture (*"the invisible things of God"*) intensifies the language of the French Confession (1559), which was written by Calvin, along with Beza and Peter Viret, and which, in its second article, speaks more generally of Creation as a location of divine revelation. See Arthur C. Cochrane, *Reformed Confessions of the Sixteenth Century* (Philadelphia: Westminster Press, 1966), 189–90 and 144.

2. Walter Brueggemann, *In Man We Trust: The Neglected Side of Biblical Faith* (Richmond, Va.: John Knox Press, 1972), 66. Brueggemann calls the court theologians of tenth-century

Israel "Renaissance Men" (61). Incidentally, Brueggemann's subtitle represents a conclusion from the perspective of the church. Wisdom was not neglected by extra-ecclesiastical religious orientations.

3. Francis Bacon, *The Advancement of Learning* (published with *New Atlantis*), ed. Arthur Johnston (Oxford: Clarendon Press, 1974), 40.

4. Francis Bacon, *New Atlantis*, in ibid., 229 (Bacon's emphasis).

5. *The Advancement of Learning*, 1.6.10, p. 39. Bacon here is quoting Job 26:7 ("He stretcheth out the north over the empty space, and hangeth the earth upon nothing").

6. *The Advancement of Learning*, 1.6.16, p. 42.

7. Francis Bacon, *The New Organon and Related Writings*, ed. Fulton H. Anderson (New York: Liberal Arts Press, 1960), 1.89, p. 89.

8. Francis Bacon, *Valerius Terminus of the Interpretation of Nature with the Annotations of Hermes Stella* (London, 1603), 221.

9. *The Advancement of Learning*, 1.4.3, p. 26; 1.5.8, p. 35; 1.6.16, p. 42.

10. Ibid., 1.6.11, pp. 40–41.

11. Francis Bacon, "The Great Instauration," in *The New Organon and Related Writings*, ed. Anderson, 29 (emphasis added).

12. *The New Organon*, 1.97, p. 94.

13. "The Great Instauration," 21.

14. *The Advancement of Learning*, 2.7.6, p. 93.

15. Ibid., 1.3.3, p. 19.

16. Ibid., 1.5.11, p. 36.

17. "The Great Instauration," 23.

18. *The Advancement of Learning*, 1.6.16, p. 42.

19. John Dillenberger dates this shift to the middle of the eighteenth century by making Christian Wolff a key spokesman for it. He comments that, since clarity was a criterion for knowledge, Wolff was able to make knowledge derived from nature superior to knowledge derived from Scripture. Perhaps if clarity is the chief or sole criterion for measuring the value of knowledge, the eighteenth century becomes a crucial time, but the exchange of priorities is much earlier. I see it already in Bacon and in the birth of modern science. John Dillenberger, *Protestant Thought and Natural Science* (Notre Dame, Ind.: University of Notre Dame Press, 1960), 169.

20. *The Advancement of Learning*, 1.4.12, p. 32.

21. Ibid., 1.8.6, p. 58.

22. John Locke, *An Essay Concerning Human Understanding*, ed. Alexander Campbell Fraser (Oxford: Clarendon Press, 1894), 1:123 (bk. 2, chap. 1, 2).

23. Ibid., 2:421 (bk. 4, chap. 18, 5); 2:423 (bk. 4, chap. 18, 8); 2:438 (bk. 4, chap. 19, 14). The annotator adds that this "reason" is full, including spiritual with sensuous constituents, but in the passages before there can be no doubt that what is natural is being used as a control on what can be taken as spiritual with the certainty of faith.

24. Ibid., 2:440 (bk. 4, chap. 19, 16).

25. John Locke, "The Reasonableness of Christianity, as delivered in the Scriptures," in *The Works of John Locke* (London: T. Longman et al., 1794), 6:5.

26. Ibid., 82.

27. See "An Essay for the Understanding of St. Paul's Epistles by Consulting St. Paul Himself," in *The Works of John Locke*, vol. 7, esp. xix.

28. Richard Ashcraft, "Faith and Knowledge in Locke's Philosophy," in *John Locke: Problems and Perspectives*, ed. John W. Yolton (Cambridge: Cambridge University Press, 1969), 214; see generally 194–223.

29. John W. Yolton, *John Locke and the Way of Ideas* (Oxford: Oxford University Press, 1956), 117.

30. Thomas Paine, *The Age of Reason, Being an Investigation of True and Fabulous Theology* (1794–95; reprint, New York: Prometheus Books, 1984), 33.

31. Ibid., 185.

32. Ibid., 31.

33. Ibid., 38, 39, 186–87.

34. Ibid., 42, 24.

35. Ibid., 24–25, 185.

36. J.G.A. Pocock, *The Ancient Constitution and the Feudal Law: A Study of English Historical Thought in the Seventeenth Century* (Cambridge: Cambridge University Press, 1957), 4, 9–10, and 29. I am intrigued by the influence this legal interest and distinction in history might have had on Calvin's understanding of the history of Israel, given his own legal training and his own subtle attempt to value that history highly, to see its distance and difference from his present, and to see continuities between his present and that past.

37. Hans W. Frei, *The Eclipse of Biblical Narrative: A Study in Eighteenth- and Nineteenth-Century Hermeneutics* (New Haven: Yale University Press, 1974), 48–50.

38. *The New Science of Giambattista Vico*, trans. Thomas Goddard Bergin and Max Harold Fisch (Ithaca, N.Y.: Cornell University Press, 1948), pars. 359, 383, and 499 on pp. 94, 108, and 151.

39. Ibid., par. 51, p. 31.

40. Ibid., par. 331, p. 85.

41. Ibid., par. 429, p. 124.

42. "Wisdom is the faculty which commands all the disciplines by which we acquire all the sciences and arts that make up humanity." Ibid. "True wisdom, then, should teach the knowledge of divine things in order to conduct human things to the highest good." Ibid., par. 364, p. 98.

43. Ibid., par. 178, p. 63.

44. Ibid., par. 130, p. 55.

45. Ibid., par. 310, p. 81.

46. Ibid., pars. 133 and 2 on pp. 56 and 4.

47. For some of the more important instances, see ibid., pars. 2, 145, 161, 237, 241, 245, 333, 366, 631, and 922ff. on pp. 3–4, 57, 60, 70, 70, 71, 86, 99, 211, and 304ff.

48. This is Vico's concluding injunction. See ibid., par. 1112, p. 383.

49. By concluding that "Vico's remarks about the role of providence in its immanent and transcendent senses represent an attempt to present what is basically a naturalistic theory in a religious light," Leon Pompa shows himself to be one of many commentators who dismiss the theological and scriptural interests of Vico as unnecessary scaffolding. Pompa refers favorably—although he admits the position is extreme—to an essay by F. Vaughan in which Vaughan argues that the theological in Vico is a deliberate ruse and concealment. Leon Pompa, *Vico: A Study of the 'New Science'* (Cambridge: Cambridge University Press, 1975), 60; for the reference to Vaughan, see 190. It is interesting to note that as transitional figures both Vico and Locke are objects of this kind of treatment, that is, having their theological commitments discounted as irrelevant to their intellectual interests and scholarly contributions.

50. Georg Wilhelm Friedrich Hegel, *The Philosophy of History*, trans. J. Sibree (New York: Willey Book Co., 1944), 13.

51. Ibid., 15, 457.

52. Ibid., 60.

53. Mark C. Taylor, *Altarity* (Chicago: University of Chicago Press, 1987), 11.

54. *The Philosophy of History*, 24.

55. Ibid., 41.

56. Ibid., 52.

57. Ibid., 418.

58. Julius Wellhausen, *Prolegomena to the History of Ancient Israel* (New York: Meridian Books, 1957), 10.

59. Ibid., 398.

60. Ibid., 353.

61. Ibid., 412.

62. Ibid., 420–22.

63. See Moshe Weinfeld, "Israelite Religion," in *Religions of Antiquity*, ed. Robert M. Seltzer (New York: Macmillan, 1990), 96–121.

64. *Prolegomena*, 422–23.

65. Ibid., 412.

66. Ferdinand Christian Baur, *The Church History of the First Three Centuries*, trans. Allan Menzies (1853; reprint, London: Williams & Norgate, 1878), 49.

67. See Zvi Rosen, *Bruno Bauer and Karl Marx* (The Hague: Martinus Nijhoff, 1977).

68. Adolf Harnack, *History of Dogma*, vol. 1, trans. Neil Buchanan (Boston: Roberts Brothers, 1895), esp. 281–85; see also the appendix on Jewish Christianity, 287–317.

69. Albert Schweitzer, *The Mystery of the Kingdom of God*, trans. Walter Lowrie (New York: Bodd, Mead & Co., 1914), 274–75.

70. See J. C. O'Neill, *The Bible's Authority: A Portrait Gallery of Thinkers from Lessing to Bultmann* (Edinburgh: T. and T. Clark, 1991), esp. 305–7.

71. Jane Tompkins, "The Reader in History: The Changing Shape of Literary Response," in *Reader-Response Criticism: From Formalism to Post-Structuralism*, ed. Jane Tompkins (Baltimore, Md.: Johns Hopkins University Press, 1980), 201–32.

72. Immanuel Kant, *The Critique of Judgement*, trans. James Creed Meredith (1928; reprint, Oxford: Clarendon Press, 1986), 91.

73. Alan Lazaroff argues that implicit in Kant's analysis is a sublime that must be seen as a religious feeling with particularly powerful consequences for moral ideas. See his "Kantian Sublime: Aesthetic Judgement and Religious Feeling," in *Immanuel Kant: Critical Assessments*, ed. Ruth F. Chadwick and Clive Cazeaux (London: Routledge, 1992), 356–77.

74. Ibid., 210–12.

75. While I take responsibility for the particular and perhaps questionable shape I have given to Kant, due in part to my interest in relating him to Coleridge, I do want to acknowledge my appreciation of a number of excellent commentaries on Kant, works that made me far more aware than I otherwise would have been of the difficulties in Kant's project and of the uncertainties that his treatment of the aesthetic creates: Mary A. McCloskey, *Kant's Aesthetic* (Albany: State University of New York Press, 1987); Chadwick and Cazeaux, eds., *Immanuel Kant: Critical Assessments*, 88–395; Eva Schaper, "Taste, Sublimity, and Genius: The Aesthetics of Nature and Art," in *The Cambridge Companion to Kant*, ed. Paul Guyer (Cambridge: Cambridge University Press, 1992), 367–93; and Donald W. Crawford, *Kant's Aesthetic Theory* (Madison: University of Wisconsin Press, 1974). I depart from standard commentaries on Kant's aesthetics in not giving an account of such judgments in terms of the four defining aspects, namely, that they are disinterested, that they are related to the perception of form, that they are necessary, and that they are universal. This last aspect, of course, is taken as most characteristic of the preceding critiques, since universality is a warranting claim for synthetic a priori knowledge and for synthetic a priori moral judgments. I think that disinterestedness and perception of form are crucial to Kant's critique of aesthetic judgments, but I am not so sure that necessity and universality are. They seem to have their place more from reasons of formal symmetry with the preceding critiques. In any event, I think that it is unfortunate to set the whole of Kant's aesthetics on the point of universality in aesthetic judgments. That they are and need to be shared is obviously important, but it may be possible to allow this aspect of aesthetic judgments to be more culturally and historically determined; indeed, since Kant fails, in my

opinion, to make them universal, his failure may dictate such an alternative position. He would stress, however, the universality of the capacity of aesthetic pleasure, and since he has so high a regard for it, cultural modesty would dictate that this capacity not be claimed for oneself alone.

76. Samuel Taylor Coleridge, *Biographia Literaria; or, Biographical Sketches of My Literary Life and Opinions* (New York: Harper & Brothers, 1853), 155.

77. "The writings of the illustrious sage of Koenigsberg, the founder of the Critical Philosophy, more than any other work, at once invigorated and disciplined my understanding. The originality, the depth, yet solidity and importance of the distinctions; the adamantine chain of the logic; and I will venture to add . . . the clearness and evidence of the Critique of the Pure Reason; and Critique of the Judgment; of the Metaphysical Elements of Natural Philosophy; and of his Religion within the bounds of Pure Reason, took possession of me as with a giant's hand. After fifteen years' familiarity with them, I still read these and all his other productions with undiminished delight and increasing admiration." Ibid., 257.

78. Ibid., 201.

79. Ibid., 231, 237, and 248.

80. Ibid., 335 and 341.

81. Ibid., 347–48 and 353.

82. Ibid., 363–64.

83. Ibid., 259 and 272.

84. Ibid., 405.

85. Ibid., 429.

86. "[I]n the Bible is more that *finds* me than I have experienced in all other books put together; that the words of the Bible find me at greater depths of my being; and that whatever finds me brings with it an irresistible evidence of its having proceeded from the Holy Spirit." Samuel Taylor Coleridge, *Confessions of an Inquiring Spirit* (London: Adam & Charles Black, 1956), 43.

87. Lionel Trilling, *Matthew Arnold* (New York: W. W. Norton, 1939), vii—xiv.

88. Matthew Arnold, *Culture and Anarchy: An Essay in Political and Social Criticism* (London: Macmillan, 1903). While Arnold mentions the demonstrations in Hyde Park that occurred in July 1866 particularly (pp. 55 and 72, e.g.), it is a mistake to conclude, I think, that for him anarchy is related to the interests of the working class and that culture is a construct that can be appropriated by the ruling class as a justification for its power. He takes the demonstrations as symptomatic of polarization and the individualization of interests, as symptomatic of a loss of the cultural sense of interests in common. One could argue that he is as hard on aristocrats for their superficiality, or "barbarism," and the middle class for its "philistine" attitudes as he is on the working class.

89. Matthew Arnold, "The Function of Criticism at the Present Time," in *Essays in Criticism* (London: Macmillan, 1903), 1–44, and idem, *Culture and Anarchy*.

90. "The Function of Criticism at the Present Time," 20.

91. Matthew Arnold, "Literature and Dogma: An Essay Towards a Better Apprehension of the Bible," in *Dissent and Dogma*, ed. R. H. Super (Ann Arbor: University of Michigan Press, 1968), 139–411. For the identification of culture with reading texts other than the Bible in order to allow the Bible to be read in a culturally beneficial way, see 152–57.

92. Ibid., 162.

93. *Culture and Anarchy*, 76. Arnold wants very much to identify the state not as a particular interest and power but as the expression of the collective, of that which people, regardless of their positions in society, have in common, especially that which allows them to transcend particular interests and immediate gains for the "national right reason" (ibid., 78).

94. Ibid., xvii and 11.

95. See the many references to Proverbs on pages 180 and 205, for example.

96. "Literature and Dogma," 205.

97. Ibid., 182.

98. Ibid., 250.

99. I. A. Richards, *Principles of Literary Criticism* (New York: Harcourt, Brace & Co., 1925), 32–33.

100. Cleanth Brooks, *The Well Wrought Urn: Studies in the Structure of Poetry* (New York: Harcourt, Brace & World, 1947), 216–17 and 256.

101. W. K. Wimsatt Jr., *The Verbal Icon: Studies in the Meaning of Poetry* (Lexington: University of Kentucky Press, 1954), 231.

Chapter 3

1. Linda Hutcheon, *A Poetics of Postmodernism: History, Theory, Fiction* (New York: Routledge, 1988), 29 and 34–35.

2. Ibid., 75.

3. Robert Venturi et al., *Learning from Las Vegas: The Forgotten Symbolism of Architectural Form* (Cambridge: MIT Press, 1977), 52.

4. See, for example, Ernesto Laclau and Chantal Mouffe, *Hegemony and Socialist Strategy: Towards a Radical Democratic Politics* (London: Verso, 1987), 149–93.

5. Chris Weedon, *Feminist Practice and Poststructuralist Theory* (Oxford: Basil Blackwell, 1987), 35.

6. Henry L. Gates Jr., "Writing 'Race' and the Difference It Makes," in *"Race," Writing, and Difference*, ed. Henry L Gates Jr. (Chicago: University of Chicago Press, 1986), 1–20.

7. Anthony Appiah, "The Uncompleted Argument: Du Bois and the Illusion of Race," in *"Race," Writing, and Difference*, ed. Gates, 21–37.

8. Frank Lentricchia, *Criticism and Social Change* (Chicago: University of Chicago Press, 1983), 19.

9. Scott Lash and John Urry, *The End of Organized Capitalism* (Cambridge: Polity Press, 1987), 292.

10. Jacques Derrida, "Structure, Sign, and Play in the Discourse of the Human Sciences," in *The Languages of Criticism and the Sciences of Man: The Structuralist Controversy*, ed. Richard Macksey and Eugenio Donato (Baltimore, Md.: Johns Hopkins University Press, 1970), 271; see generally 247–72. See also *Writing and Difference*, trans. Alan Bass (Chicago: University of Chicago Press, 1978).

11. Venturi, *Learning from Las Vegas*, 6.

12. Richard Harland, *Superstructuralism: The Philosophy of Structuralism and Post-Structuralism* (London: Methuen, 1987), 62.

13. Fredric Jameson, *Postmodernism, or, The Culture of Late Capitalism* (Durham, N.C.: Duke University Press, 1991), 44–46.

14. Jean Baudrillard, *America*, trans. Chris Turner (London: Verso, 1988).

15. Jean-François Lyotard, *The Postmodernist Condition: A Report on Knowledge*, trans. Geoff Bennington and Brian Massumi (Minneapolis: University of Minnesota Press, 1979), 37.

16. Edith Wyschogrod, *Saints and Postmodernism: Revisioning Moral Philosophy* (Chicago: University of Chicago Press, 1990), xviii.

17. Fredric Jameson, "Postmodernism or the Cultural Logic of Late Capitalism," *New Left Review*, no. 146 (1984): 64.

18. See Pierre Bourdieu, *Distinction: A Social Critique of the Judgement of Taste*, trans. Richard Nice (Cambridge: Harvard University Press, 1984).

19. Barbara Herrnstein Smith, *Contingencies of Value: Alternative Perspectives for Critical Theory* (Cambridge: Harvard University Press, 1988), 100.

20. Ibid., 146.

21. Ibid., 15, 42, and 33.

22. Ibid., 13.

23. Ibid., 42 and 101.

24. Ibid., 47, 50, 74, and 98.

25. Ibid., 135–39.

26. Ibid., 30.

27. Ibid., 169.

28. Ibid., 147, 148.

29. Ibid., 111–12.

30. Ibid., 144.

31. Ibid., 47–50 and 74.

32. Ibid., 40.

33. Ibid., 32.

34. Stanley Fish, *Doing What Comes Naturally: Change, Rhetoric, and the Practice of Theory in Literary and Legal Studies* (Durham, N.C.: Duke University Press, 1989), 83, 235.

35. Stanley Fish, *Is There a Text in This Class? The Authority of Interpretive Communities* (Cambridge: Harvard University Press, 1980), 13; see also 168.

36. Ibid., 172–73, 241.

37. *Doing What Comes Naturally*, 97.

38. Ibid., 83.

39. Ibid., 459–60.

40. *Is There a Text in this Class?* 332.

41. Stanley Fish, "Normal Circumstances, Literal Language, Direct Speech Acts, the Ordinary, the Everyday, the Obvious, What Goes Without Saying, and Other Special Cases," in *Interpretive Social Sciences: A Reader,* ed. Paul Rabinow and William M. Sullivan (Berkeley and Los Angeles: University of California Press, 1979), 265.

42. *Doing What Comes Naturally*, 26.

43. *Is There a Text in this Class?* 336.

44. *Doing What Comes Naturally*, 12, 521, 483.

45. See, for example, Stanley Fish, "Freedom of Speech: No Such Thing and It's a Good Thing Too," *Faculty Newsletter* 5, no. 5 (1994): 1–5.

46. *Is There a Text in this Class?* 320.

47. *Doing What Comes Naturally*, 246.

48. Ibid., 462.

49. Ibid., 467.

50. Ibid., 156.

51. Ibid., 146.

52. See, for example, Steven Connor, *Theory and Cultural Value* (Oxford: Basil Blackwell, 1992), 32.

53. Wyschogrod, *Saints and Postmodernism*, 150.

54. Ibid., 226.

55. Ibid., 13, 161, and 17.

56. Ibid., 243.

57. Simon Critchley, *The Ethics of Deconstruction: Derrida and Levinas* (Oxford: Basil Blackwell, 1992), 42.

58. Ibid., 8.

59. Ibid., 156.

60. Ibid., 168.
61. Ibid., 238.

Chapter 4

1. Maurice Blanchot, *The Infinite Conversation* (L'entretien infini), trans. Susan Hanson (Minneapolis: University of Minnesota Press, 1993), 13.
2. Ibid., 349.
3. Ibid., 400–401.
4. Ibid., 89–90.
5. Maurice Blanchot, *The Writing of the Disaster* (L'écriture du desastre), trans. Ann Smock (Lincoln: University of Nebraska Press, 1986), 107.
6. Ibid., 116–17.
7. *The Infinite Conversation*, 28 and 163.
8. Ibid., 43.
9. Ibid., 340.
10. Ibid., 207.
11. Ibid., 145.
12. Ibid., 339.
13. Ibid., 42.
14. Maurice Blanchot, *The Space of Literature* (Espace littiraire), trans. Ann Smock (Lincoln: University of Nebraska Press, 1982), 137.
15. *The Infinite Conversation*, xi.
16. Maurice Blanchot, *The Step Not Beyond* (Le pas au-dela), trans. Lycett Nelvon (Albany: State University of New York Press, 1973), 104.
17. *The Space of Literature*, 174.
18. *The Infinite Conversation*, 319.
19. Ibid., 50.
20. *The Step Not Beyond*, 91.
21. Maurice Blanchot, *The Gaze of Orpheus and Other Literary Essays*, trans. Lydia Davis (Barrytown, N.Y.: Station Hill Press, 1981), 5.
22. *The Infinite Conversation*, 12.
23. Ibid., 16.
24. Ibid., 23.
25. *The Gaze of Orpheus and Other Literary Essays*, 36–37.
26. *The Writing of Disaster*, 31.
27. *The Space of Literature*, 240.
28. *The Infinite Conversation*, 86.
29. Ibid., 128.
30. Ibid., 129.
31. Ibid., 233.
32. *The Step Not Beyond*, 60.
33. *The Space of Literature*, 5.
34. Ibid., 30.
35. *The Infinite Conversation*, 242.
36. *The Step Not Beyond*, 38.
37. *The Writing of the Disaster*, 65.
38. Michel Foucault and Maurice Blanchot, *Foucault/Blanchot*, trans. Jeffrey Mehlmann and Brian Massumi (New York: Zone Books, 1987), 22.

39. Maurice Blanchot, "The Beast of Lascaux," trans. David Paul, in *René Char's Poetry* (1953; reprint, Rome: Editions De Luca, 1956), 30.

40. *The Space of Literature*, 26.

41. *The Infinite Conversation*, 49.

42. Ibid., 126.

43. Ibid., 127.

44. Ibid., 256.

45. Ibid., 308.

46. *The Writing of the Disaster*, 30.

47. *The Space of Literature*, 61.

48. Ibid., 128.

49. Ibid., 238.

50. *The Infinite Conversation*, 205.

51. Ibid., 53.

52. *Foucault/Blanchot*, 27.

53. *The Infinite Conversation*, 44.

54. Ibid., 48 and 65, for example.

55. Ibid., 431.

56. *The Writing of the Disaster*, 51.

57. *The Space of Literature*, 33.

58. Ibid., 60.

59. Ibid., 121.

60. Ibid., 264.

61. *The Step Not Beyond*, 114, and *The Writing of the Disaster*, 2 and 7.

62. *The Step Not Beyond*, 97.

63. *The Writing of the Disaster*, 15.

64. Ibid., 39.

65. Ibid., 101.

66. *The Space of Literature*, 204.

67. *The Infinite Conversation*, 77–78.

68. *The Step Not Beyond*, 50.

69. "The Beast of Lascaux," 31.

70. *The Space of Literature*, 30.

71. *The Step Not Beyond*, 64.

72. *The Infinite Conversation*, 215.

73. *The Writing of the Disaster*, 19.

74. *The Infinite Conversation*, 60.

75. Ibid., 30.

76. Ibid., 215.

77. *The Space of Literature*, 258.

78. Ibid., 34.

79. *The Infinite Conversation*, 26.

80. "The Beast of Lascaux," 33.

81. *The Space of Literature*, 140.

82. Ibid., 141.

83. Ibid., 153.

84. *The Infinite Conversation*, 400.

85. Julia Kristeva, *Powers of Horror: An Essay on Abjection*, trans. Leon S. Roudiez (New York: Columbia University Press, 1982), 3, 5, 15.

86. Ibid., 88.

87. Ibid., 121.

88. Julia Kristeva, *Tales of Love*, trans. Leon S. Roudiez (New York: Columbia University Press, 1987), 33.

89. Ibid., 115.

90. Julia Kristeva, *In the Beginning Was Love: Psychoanalysis and Faith*, trans. Arthur Goldhammer (New York: Columbia University Press, 1987), 9 and 17.

91. Ibid., 61.

92. Julia Kristeva, *Desire in Language: A Semiotic Approach to Literature and Art*, trans. Thomas Gora et al. (New York: Columbia University Press, 1980), 97–120.

93. *Tales of Love*, 279 and 294.

94. Toril Moi, introduction to *The Kristeva Reader*, ed. Toril Moi (Oxford: Basil Blackwell, 1986), 18.

95. Julia Kristeva, "The System and the Speaking Subject," in *The Kristeva Reader*, ed. Moi, 32.

96. Julia Kristeva, "Women's Time," trans. Alice Jardine and Harry Blake, in *The Kristeva Reader*, ed. Moi, 196.

97. *Desire in Language*, 125.

98. Julia Kristeva, *Black Sun: Depression and Melancholia*, trans. Leon S. Roudiez (New York: Columbia University Press, 1989), 110; see also 122.

99. Ibid., 190.

CONCLUSION

1. George A. Lindbeck, *The Nature of Doctrine: Religion and Theology in a Postliberal Age* (Philadelphia: Westminster Press, 1984). See my response to this book in *Bound to Differ: The Dynamics of Theological Discourses* (University Park: Pennsylvania State University Press, 1992), 37–40.

2. Garrett Green, "'The Bible as . . .': Fictional Narrative and Scriptural Truth," in *Scriptural Authority and Narrative Interpretation*, ed. Garrett Green (Philadelphia: Fortress Press, 1987), 79–96.

3. See Hans Vaihinger, *The Philosophy of "As If": A System of the Theoretical, Practical, and Religious Fictions of Mankind*, trans. C. K. Ogden (New York: Harcourt, Brace & Co., 1924), and Frank Kermode, *The Sense of an Ending: Studies in the Theory of Fiction* (New York: Oxford University Press, 1967).

4. David H. Kelsey, *The Uses of Scripture in Recent Theology* (Philadelphia: Fortress Press, 1975).

5. Donald K. McKim, *What Christians Believe About the Bible* (Nashville, Tenn.: T. Nelson, 1985).

6. See M. Basil Pennington, *Centering Prayer: Renewing an Ancient Christian Prayer Form* (Garden City, N.Y.: Doubleday, 1982).

7. Mark C. Taylor, *Erring: A Postmodernist A/theology* (Chicago: University of Chicago Press, 1984). See also my response to this important book in *Bound to Differ*, 39–41.

8. See Wesley A. Kort, *Story, Text, and Scripture: Literary Interests in Biblical Narrative* (University Park: Pennsylvania State University Press, 1988), 40–49 and 94–96.

9. Julia Kristeva, "Romeo and Juliet: Love-Hatred in the Couple," in *Tales of Love*, trans. Leon S. Roudiez (New York: Columbia University Press, 1987), 209–33.

10. Rosemary Radford Ruether, *Sexism and God-Talk: Toward a Feminist Theology* (Boston: Beacon Press, 1983), 23.

11. Alicia Suskin Ostriker, *Feminist Revision and the Bible* (Oxford: Basil Blackwell, 1993), 27–50.

INDEX

TM 8199·

15